Writing the Critical Essay

Illegal Immigration

An OPPOSING VIEWPOINTS® Guide

Writing the Critical Essay

Illegal Immigration

An OPPOSING VIEWPOINTS® Guide

Other books in the Writing the Critical Essay series:

Abortion
Alcohol
Animal Rights
Assisted Suicide
Cloning
The Death Penalty
Eating Disorders
Energy Alternatives
Global Warming
Marijuana
The Patriot Act
Prisons
Racism
School Violence
Terrorism

Writing the Cri...

Illegal Immigration

An **OPPOSING VIEWPOINTS®** Guide

Laura K. Egendorf, *Book Editor*

Christine Nasso, *Publisher*
Elizabeth Des Chenes, *Managing Editor*

OPPOSING VIEWPOINTS® SERIES

GREENHAVEN PRESS
An imprint of Thomson Gale, a part of The Thomson Corporation

THOMSON
GALE

Detroit • New York • San Francisco • New Haven, Conn. • Waterville, Maine • London

THOMSON

——————★——————TM

GALE

LIBRARY OF CONGRESS CATALOGING-IN-PUBLICATION DATA
Illegal immigration / Laura K. Egendorf, book editor.   p. cm. — (Writing the critical essay) Includes bibliographical references and index. ISBN-13: 978-0-7377-3582-6 (hardcover) ISBN-10: 0-7377-3582-1 (hardcover) 1. United States—Emigration and immigration. 2. Immigrants—United States. I. Egendorf, Laura K., 1973- JV6465.I45 2007 304.8'73—dc22
2006033097

Printed in the United States of America

Foreword   9

Introduction   11
   Background to Controversy: Immigration and Illegal
   Immigration: Important Differences

Section One: Opposing Viewpoints on Illegal Immigration

   Viewpoint One: Illegal Immigrants Take Jobs from
   Americans   18
     Steven A. Camarota

   Viewpoint Two: Illegal Immigrants Do Not Take Jobs
   from Americans   25
     Adam Davidson

   Viewpoint Three: Illegal Immigrants Do Not Respect
   American Values   31
     Pat Buchanan

   Viewpoint Four: Illegal Immigrants Embody American
   Values   36
     Jeff Jacoby

   Viewpoint Five: Illegal Immigration Has a Negative
   Effect on the U.S. Health Care System   42
     Federation for American Immigration Reform

   Viewpoint Six: Illegal Immigration Does Not Have a
   Negative Effect on the U.S. Health Care System   49
     Richard J. Gonzales

Section Two: Model Essays and Writing Exercises

   Preface A: The Five-Paragraph Essay   56

   Preface B: The Cause-and-Effect Essay   58

Essay One: What Causes Illegal Immigration? 61
  Exercise A: Create an Outline from an Existing
        Essay 65

Essay Two: Illegal Immigration: Criminalizing America 66
  Exercise A: Create an Outline from an Existing Essay 70
  Exercise B: Organize and Write Your Own Five-
        Paragraph Cause-and-Effect Essay 71

Essay Three: Imagining Amnesty for Illegal Immigrants:
A Bad Solution to a Growing Problem 73
  Exercise A: Examining Introductions and Conclusions 79
  Exercise B: Using Quotations to Enliven Your Essay 81

Final Writing Challenge: Write Your Own
Five-Paragraph Cause-and-Effect Essay 83

Section Three: Supporting Research Material

  Appendix A: Facts About Illegal Immigration 88

  Appendix B: Finding and Using Sources of
  Information 92

  Appendix C: Using MLA Style to Create a
  Works-Cited List 96

  Appendix D: Sample Essay Topics 98

  Organizations to Contact 99

  Bibliography 104

  Index 108

  Picture Credits 111

  About the Editor 112

Examining the state of writing and how it is taught in the United States was the official purpose of the National Commission on Writing in America's Schools and Colleges. The commission, made up of teachers, school administrators, business leaders, and college and university presidents, released its first report in 2003. "Despite the best efforts of many educators," commissioners argued, "writing has not received the full attention it deserves." Among the findings of the commission was that most fourth-grade students spent less than three hours a week writing, that three-quarters of high school seniors never receive a writing assignment in their history or social studies classes, and that more than 50 percent of first-year students in college have problems writing error-free papers. The commission called for a "cultural sea change" that would increase the emphasis on writing for both elementary and secondary schools. These conclusions have made some educators realize that writing must be emphasized in the curriculum. As colleges are demanding an ever-higher level of writing proficiency from incoming students, schools must respond by making students more competent writers. In response to these concerns, the SAT, an influential standardized test used for college admissions, required an essay for the first time in 2005.

Books in the Writing the Critical Essay: An Opposing Viewpoints Guide series use the patented Opposing Viewpoints format to help students learn to organize ideas and arguments and to write essays using common critical writing techniques. Each book in the series focuses on a particular type of essay writing—including expository, persuasive, descriptive, and narrative—that students learn while being taught both the five-paragraph essay as well as longer pieces of writing that have an opinionated focus. These guides include everything necessary to help students research, outline, draft, edit, and ultimately write successful essays across the curriculum, including essays for the SAT.

Using Opposing Viewpoints

This series is inspired by and builds upon Greenhaven Press's acclaimed Opposing Viewpoints series. As in the parent series, each book in the Writing the Critical Essay series focuses on a timely and controversial social issue that provides lots of opportunities for creating thought-provoking essays. The first section of each volume begins with a brief introductory essay that provides context for the opposing viewpoints that follow. These articles are chosen for their accessibility and clearly stated views. The thesis of each article is made explicit in the article's title and is accentuated by its pairing with an opposing or alternative view. These essays are both models of persuasive writing techniques and valuable research material that students can mine to write their own informed essays. Guided reading and discussion questions help lead students to key ideas and writing techniques presented in the selections.

The second section of each book begins with a preface discussing the format of the essays and examining characteristics of the featured essay type. Model five-paragraph and longer essays then demonstrate that essay type. The essays are annotated so that key writing elements and techniques are pointed out to the student. Sequential, step-by-step exercises help students construct and refine thesis statements; organize material into outlines; analyze and try out writing techniques; write transitions, introductions, and conclusions; and incorporate quotations and other researched material. Ultimately, students construct their own compositions using the designated essay type.

The third section of each volume provides additional research material and writing prompts to help the student. Additional facts about the topic of the book serve as a convenient source of supporting material for essays. Other features help students go beyond the book for their research. Like other Greenhaven Press books, each book in the Writing the Critical Essay series includes bibliographic listings of relevant periodical articles, books, Web sites, and organizations to contact.

Writing the Critical Essay: An Opposing Viewpoints Guide will help students master essay techniques that can be used in any discipline.

Background to Controversy: Immigration and Illegal Immigration: Important Differences

One of the enduring clichés about the United States is that it is a "melting pot," a nation of immigrants from around the world joining to form one society. While immigration has always been part of U.S. history, not everyone who comes to live in America does so legally. In 2006, 11 million people were illegal residents, a number that grows by more than four hundred thousand each year. By comparison, in 2005 more than 1 million people were granted permanent residence status. A central question to the issue of illegal immigration is: Why do people immigrate illegally when legal entrance into the United States is possible? Furthermore, what prompts the decision to immigrate illegally and how do these immigrants reach the United States?

Entering Legally

Illegal immigration persists because, although legal immigration into the United States is possible, it is largely restricted to four groups. The easiest way to become a legal U.S. resident is to be related to one. Fifty-eight percent of the people who are given permanent residence status are the relatives of citizens or other permanent residents. Immediate relatives, such as spouses, parents, and minor children qualify, as do secondary relatives (siblings and adult children). The next option is to be sponsored by a U.S.-based employer. Immigrants who receive legal status through this method are often required to work in fields for which there is a high demand for jobs, such as nurses and college professors, or to be extraordinarily talented. As a writer for Forbes.com details, "Artists and athletes can get in with virtually no hold-up. But you can't just brag your way into the U.S. There's a checklist of 10 criteria that qualify you as uniquely skilled. Among the criteria: winning top-notch awards; . . . working for an organization with a distinguished reputation . . . and participating in well-established athletic competitions."[1] Political refugees from certain countries are a third group that can become permanent legal residents. The immigrants who benefit the most from this designation are the Cubans, whose Communist government has long been opposed by the United States. Finally, if a potential immigrant does not meet any of these three requirements, the only other legal option is to win one of the fifty thousand visas awarded in an annual lottery. The bulk of those visas go to immigrants from underrepresented countries, primarily the Middle East and sub-Saharan Africa.

Why They Risk It

Given the restrictions placed on legal immigration, it is perhaps not surprising that hundreds of thousands of people enter the United States illegally each year. They immigrate to America for several reasons, primarily economic and political. Perhaps the most common reason for illegal immigration is the same as for those who come legally: to better their quality of life. Although illegal immigrants are often paid below the minimum wage (because employers have no legal obligation to pay them otherwise), those wages are still typically higher than they would receive in their homeland, sometimes as much as ten times more. For example, Mexico's minimum wage is the equivalent of $4.30 per day and its per capita income is $10,000, compared to $42,000 in the United States. Illegal immigrants—and legal immigrants as well—frequently send some of their wages back to their families who still live in

the native country. In fact, remittance, which is money sent from one person to another, typically via wire transfer, is a major source of income for Mexico and many other countries. In 2005, $20 billion was remitted to Mexico from the United States, just over half of the total of $39 billion that was sent out of America that year. The effects these funds can have on the families and towns of immigrants can be enormous. According to *Los Angeles Times* staff writer Richard Boudreaux, "remittances—private aid from the poor to the poorer—offer a rare chance to accumulate savings; invest in schooling, housing or a small business; and rise into the middle class."[2]

Illegal immigrants can also have political reasons for wanting to enter the United States, although they do not always legally qualify for refugee status. The U.S. government determines which immigrants can be considered refugees based on its own foreign policy. According to the United Nations and U.S. law, a refugee is a person who cannot return to his or her native land out of fear of persecution, be it religious, racial, or political. One country whose citizens rarely qualify for refugee status, despite the

An immigrant hands his papers to an employee at the U.S. consulate in Havana, Cuba, in 2006. U.S. immigrations officials returned him to Cuba from Florida.

Demonstrators in New Hampshire protest unfair treatment and detainment of Haitian refugees in 2002.

nation's violence and political upheaval, is Haiti. Haitian immigrants typically are not labeled refugees because, unlike Cubans for example, they are not viewed by the United States as living under an oppressive government. The U.S. government also considers most Haitians to be fleeing for economic and not political reasons, and therefore they do not meet the international definition of refugee. For these reasons, Haitians and citizens of other countries not considered to be refugees by the U.S. government may try and enter the country illegally.

A Dangerous Trip

Once a person decides to immigrate illegally, he or she faces a dangerous and sometimes deadly journey. Cubans and Haitians often drown trying to make the trip by boat, with capsizings sometimes taking more than two dozen lives. People trying to cross the Mexico-U.S. border frequently turn to the less-than-reliable help of smugglers known as "coyotes." According to John Pomfret, a staff writer for the *Washington Post,*

Instead of dashing across in urban areas, illegal immigrants [have] turned to paths through the deserts of eastern California, Arizona, New Mexico and Texas. They began employing "coyotes," smugglers who demanded thousands of dollars, to lead them and often traveled under hot sun with little water. More than 2,500 have died attempting such crossings in the past decade.[3]

Crossing the border without help can also be deadly; on average, 1.5 people die each day trying to reach the United States. If illegal immigrants do cross safely, they

The skull of an illegal immigrant lies north of the U.S.-Mexico border as a U.S. Border Patrol helicopter flies by. Immigrants risk their lives to come to the United States.

still face the possibility that the border patrol will arrest them. Between October 1, 2004, and September 30, 2005, border agents apprehended 1.1 million people trying to enter the United States. Ninety percent of the people arrested were deported to their home country from where they would often repeat their journey.

Despite the dangers, hundreds of thousands of people continue to enter the United States illegally every year in the hope of improving their lives and perhaps one day becoming legal residents or even citizens. Regardless of why illegal immigration occurs, it is one of the most controversial issues facing America. The following topics are among those considered in *Writing the Critical Essay: Illegal Immigration*: the economic effects of illegal immigration, illegal immigrants and American values, and the impact illegal immigrants have on crime and national security. The articles and essays in this book help shed light on the many ways illegal immigration affects the United States, while skill-building exercises and discussion questions will help students craft essays on the subject.

Notes

1. Tara Weiss, "Jobs That Will Get You a U.S. Visa," Forbes.com, July 13, 2006. www.forbes.com/leadership/ 2006/07/13/leadership-careers-immigration-cx_tw_ 0713jobsthatgetyouausvisa.html.

2. Richard Boudreaux, "The Seeds of Promise," *Los Angeles Times*, April 16, 2006.

3. John Pomfret, "Despite Security and Dangers, Border Crossers Find Way North," *Washington Post*, May 18, 2006.

Section One: Opposing Viewpoints on Illegal Immigration

Illegal Immigrants Take Jobs from Americans

Steven A. Camarota

Steven A. Camarota argues in the following viewpoint that illegal immigration has negatively affected American workers. He claims that in the twenty-first century, U.S. citizens have lost a significant number of jobs to immigrants. According to Camarota, immigrants are not only taking jobs that Americans do not want, but they are also finding employment in higher-paying fields that require at least a high school diploma. He concludes that native-born workers have suffered significant job losses due to America's immigration policies.

Camarota is the director of research at the Center for Immigration Studies, an independent research institute that studies the economic and social impacts of immigration.

Consider the following questions:

1. According to Camarota, what percentage of the increase in immigrant employment was for immigrants who had more than a high school education?
2. By March 2004, how many adult illegal aliens were employed in the United States, according to the Current Population Surveys?
3. How many more native-born Americans were unemployed in 2004 compared to 2000, according to the author?

Steve A. Camarota, "A Jobless Recovery? Immigrant Gains and Native Losses," October, 2004. Reproduced by permission.

Do Illegal Immigrants Take Jobs from Americans?

Occupation	Unemployment Rate of U.S. Citizens	Illegal Share of Occupation
Farming, fishing, & forestry	12.8%	30%
Construction & extraction	11.3%	15%
Blding. cleaning & maintenance	10.5%	17%
Food preparation	9.4%	11%
Production	7.7%	8%
Transportation & moving	6.9%	6%
Personal care & service	6.3%	4%
Sales	5.3%	2%
Office & admin. support	5.0%	2%
Health care support	5.0%	4%

Steven A. Camarota, "Dropping Out: Immigrant Entry and Native Exit into the Labor Market," Center for Immigration Studies, March 2006.

The recovery from the recession of 2001 has been described as "jobless." In fact, an analysis of the latest Census Bureau data shows that between March of 2000 and March of 2004, the number of adults working actually increased, but all of the net change went to immigrant workers. The number of adult immigrants (18 years of age and older) holding a job increased by over two million between 2000 and 2004, while the number of adult natives holding a job is nearly half a million fewer. This [viewpoint] also finds that the number of adult natives who are unemployed or who have withdrawn from the labor force is dramatically higher in 2004 than it was in 2000. These findings raise the possibility that immigration has adversely affected the job prospects of native-born Americans. . . .

Not Just Menial Labor

Contrary to the perceptions of some, most of the net increase in immigrant employment was not at the very bottom of the labor market. . . . Less than 700,000 (only 30 percent) of the net increase in adult immigrant employment was among workers with less than a high school degree. About 20 percent of the net increase in immigrant employment was for those with just a high school degree, and 50 percent of the growth was for those who had an education beyond high school. With half of the net increase in immigrant employment among workers with an education beyond high school, the argument that "immigrants only take jobs Americans don't want" would seem to be incorrect. Immigrants are not simply taking jobs that require little education, pay relatively little, and are menial in nature. While it is true that a much larger share of immigrant than native workers have few years of schooling, immigration is increasing the supply of workers throughout the labor force.

[Statistics] show that the number holding a job declined by 1.4 million. . . . Some of this decline is explained by an increase of 217,000 in unemployment among native dropouts. The decline in the number of native dropouts also seems to be related to the retirement of older natives with few years of education. . . . The number of native dropouts not in the labor force went down slightly between 2000 and 2003, indicating that there was not an increase in non-work for this type of worker. Because American society has become more educated in recent decades, there has been a decline in the number of natives lacking a high school degree. Many older native-born dropouts are retiring. On the other hand, the unemployment rate of 13.3 percent and rate of non-work for native-born dropouts is dramatically higher than for other workers. By significantly increasing the supply of unskilled workers during the recession, immigration may be making it more difficult for these workers to improve their situation. While it might be reasonable to describe these jobs as ones that most American don't want, clearly there are still millions of unskilled Americans in the labor force. Given the persistently high unemployment rate and low rates of labor force participation among this population, it may make little sense to continually increase the supply of unskilled workers through immigration, especially during an economic downturn.

The number of natives with only a high school degree holding a job in 2004 was 2.2 million fewer than in 2000. Moreover, . . . the number of natives with only a high school degree who were unemployed was 885,000 higher. In addition, . . . the number of natives with only a high school degree not in the labor force was nearly 1.2 million higher. During the same time period, the number of immigrants with the same level of education holding a

Monte Wolverton. © 2006 Monte Wolverton. Reproduced by permission of Cagle Cartoons, Inc.

job increased by 438,000. There were also nearly 300,000 unemployed immigrants in 2004 in this educational category, an increase of about 100,000 from 2000. There is no question that immigration has increased the supply of this type of worker at the same time natives with only a high school degree have lost jobs. . . .

Illegal Immigrants in the Workforce

It is well established that illegal aliens do respond to government surveys such as the decennial census and the

U.S. Border Patrol agents load suspected illegal immigrants into a van to be transported to a holding facility in Texas in 2006.

Current Population Survey. While the CPS does not ask the foreign-born if they are legal residents of the United States, the Urban Institute, the former INS [Immigration and Naturalization Service], and the Census Bureau have all used socio-demographic characteristics in the data to estimate the size of the illegal population. Our preliminary estimates for the March 2004 CPS indicate that there were slightly over 9.1 million illegal aliens in the survey. It must be remembered that this estimate only includes illegal aliens captured by the March CPS, not those missed by the survey. By design this estimate is very similar to those prepared by the Census Bureau, the former INS and the Urban Institute. Although it should be obvious that there is no definitive means of determining whether a respondent in the survey is an illegal alien, this estimate is consistent with previous research. We estimate that in 2000, based on the March CPS from that year, that there were between 4.2 and 4.4 million adult illegal aliens employed in the United States and that this number had grown to between 5.4 to 5.6 million in the March 2004 CPS. This means that about half of the 2.3 million increase in the number of adult immigrants working in the United States was due to illegal immigration.

An Adverse Effect

The time period from 2000 to 2004 has been difficult for many American workers. This [viewpoint] shows that all of the employment losses during this time period have been absorbed by native-born Americans. The number of natives holding jobs in March of 2004 was half a million lower than in March of 2000 and the number unemployed was 2.3 million higher. Over the same time period, the number of immigrants holding jobs in the United States increased by 2.3 million. About half of the increase in immigrant employment is due to the growth of the illegal alien population. We find little evidence for the argument that immigrants only take jobs natives don't want. Immigrant employment gains have occurred throughout the labor market, with half of the increase among workers with education beyond high school. Moreover, looking at occupations shows that there are millions of natives employed in occupations that saw the largest influx of new immigrants.

We find some direct evidence that immigration has adversely impacted natives. Areas of the country with the largest increase in immigrant workers were, in many cases, areas that saw the most significant job losses for natives. Immigrant occupations with the largest immigrant influx tended to have the highest unemployment rates among natives. This certainly raises the very real possibility that immigration has adversely affected native employment.

Analyze the essay:

1. Camarota uses many statistics to support his arguments, but includes no quotations. Did this influence your reading of his argument? If so, in what way?
2. After reading this essay and its opposing pair, do you think Camarota overstates or understates the effect of illegal immigration on the U.S. labor market? Explain your answer.

Illegal Immigrants Do Not Take Jobs from Americans

Adam Davidson

In the following interview Adam Davidson argues that on the whole, illegal immigrants do not take jobs from American workers. He contends that most Americans would notice little difference in their weekly earnings if there were no illegal immigrant workers in the country. He also suggests that even though some jobs are taken by undocumented workers, their presence creates other types of jobs that American citizens fill. Davidson contends that if illegal immigrants did not perform their jobs, the positions would likely be taken over by machines and not American citizens.

Davidson is a business correspondent for National Public Radio, from which this interview was excerpted.

Consider the following questions:

1. What group of American citizens is most likely to be negatively impacted by illegal workers, according to the author? To what degree would they be affected?
2. What three cities are home to more than a third of all illegal immigrants, as reported by Davidson?
3. What two factors does Davidson say have a greater impact on wages and the U.S. economy than illegal immigration?

Adam Davidson, "Q&A: Illegal Immigrants and the U.S. Economy," *National Public Radio*, March 30, 2006. Reproduced by permission.

Nearly 12 million illegal immigrants are estimated to be living in the United States. The vast majority work in low-skill, low-wage jobs. More than half work in construction, manufacturing or leisure and hospitality. . . .

Americans Do Not Compete with Immigrants for Jobs

Q: What is the impact of illegal immigration on wages in the United States?

Well, for an individual, it depends on where you are, what kind of work you do and whether you have skills that illegal immigrants don't. But overall, illegal immigrants don't have a big impact on U.S. wage rates. The most respected recent studies show that most Americans would notice little difference in their paychecks if illegal immigrants

Construction workers repave a freeway in Chicago, Illinois. Many illegal immigrants work in construction and manufacturing jobs.

suddenly disappeared from the United States. That's because most Americans don't directly compete with illegal immigrants for jobs.

There is one group of Americans that would benefit from a dramatic cut in illegal immigration: high-school dropouts. Most economists agree that the wages of low-skill high-school dropouts are suppressed by somewhere between 3 percent and 8 percent because of competition from immigrants, both legal and illegal. Economists speculate that for the average high-school dropout, that would mean about a $25 a week raise if there were no job competition from immigrants.

Illegal immigrants seem to have very little impact on unemployment rates. Undocumented workers certainly do take jobs that would otherwise go to legal workers. But undocumented workers also create demand that leads to new jobs. They buy food and cars and cell phones, they get haircuts and go to restaurants. On average, there is close to no net impact on the unemployment rate.

"A Minimal Impact on Wages"

Q: But what about wages in cities like Los Angeles and Chicago, where there are many illegal immigrants? And what about wages in industries that use many undocumented workers?

More than a third of illegal immigrants live in just three cities: New York, Los Angeles and Chicago. But even in these places, economists believe there is minimal impact on wages. That's because many Americans from other parts of the country choose not to move to areas with large numbers of immigrants, because they want to avoid competing for jobs.

Even in industries with high concentrations of illegal workers—such as construction, restaurants and some

> ## Attracted to Cheap Prices
>
> Americans are not hooked on cheap labor as much as they are hooked on cheap prices. Illegal immigration is attractive because cheaper labor also leads to cheaper prices for the goods or services the cheap labor produces.
>
> Clarence Page, "Our Make-Believe Immigration Policy," *Liberal Opinion Week*, May 25, 2005, p. 20.

Migrant workers tend a flower field in California. Some argue that if illegal immigrants did not work in agriculture, workers would be replaced by machines.

parts of agriculture—the impact isn't as great as many people think. If there weren't illegal immigrants working in construction in places like Chicago and Miami, then demand for legal workers would go up, which would mean wages would rise. But very quickly, legal workers from other parts of the country would move to those cities, and wages would go back down. The net impact on wages would be relatively modest.

Illegal immigrants do often take some of the country's least attractive jobs, such as in meat packing and agriculture. If there were no undocumented workers available for those jobs, employers would likely invest in new technology, replacing workers with automation.

Immigration Has a Small Impact on American Jobs

Q: How do illegal immigrants affect the overall U.S. economy?

Illegal immigration has both negative and positive impacts on different parts of the economy. As noted above, wages for low-skilled workers go down. But that means the rest of America benefits by paying lower prices for things like restaurant meals, agricultural produce and construction. Another negative impact is on government expenditures. Since undocumented workers generally don't pay income taxes but do use schools and other government services, they are seen as a drain on government spending.

Brian Fairrington. Reproduced by permission of Cagle Cartoons, Inc.

There are places in the United States where illegal immigration has big effects (both positive and negative). But economists generally believe that when averaged over the whole economy, the effect is a small net positive. Harvard's George Borjas says the average American's wealth is increased by less than 1 percent because of illegal immigration.

The economic impact of illegal immigration is far smaller than other trends in the economy, such as the increasing use of automation in manufacturing or the growth in global trade. Those two factors have a much bigger impact on wages, prices and the health of the U.S. economy.

Analyze the essay:

1. In arguing that American jobs are not threatened by illegal immigration, Davidson concedes that some particular jobs are taken from some particular Americans. Do you think Davidson contradicts himself by saying this? Why or why not?

2. Davidson claims that illegal immigration has little impact on the wages or unemployment of American citizens. How do you think Steven A. Camarota, the author of the previous viewpoint, might react to this claim? What points of evidence might he use to support his argument? Support your answer using information from the text.

Illegal Immigrants Do Not Respect American Values

Pat Buchanan

Illegal immigration is helping to make the United States a Third World country, Pat Buchanan asserts in the following viewpoint. Buchanan suggests that immigrants have no interest in learning about America's history or adopting its values. Instead, he charges, they maintain their birth country's language and culture, which prevents them from assimilating into American culture. He warns that as native-born white Americans become a minority, the United States will become a disconnected group of minorities with no patriotic loyalty.

Buchanan is a nationally syndicated conservative columnist. He is the author of *State of Emergency: How Illegal Immigration Is Destroying America.*

Consider the following questions:

1. According to Buchanan, what percentage of Americans in 1960 was white?
2. In the author's view, how do academic elites perceive America?
3. What is the view of the majority of Americans toward immigration, according to Buchanan?

In 1960, when JFK [John Fitzgerald Kennedy] defeated [Richard] Nixon, America was a nation of 160 million, 90 percent white and 10 percent black, with a few million Hispanics and Asians sprinkled among us.

We were one nation, one people. We worshipped the same God, spoke the same English language, studied American history and English literature, honored the same heroes, read the same books, watched the same TV shows, went to the same movies, and saw ourselves as defenders of Western civilization against the godless communism of the Soviet Empire. . . .

An Unrecognizable America

That was yesterday. But due to the Immigration Act of 1965 and the cultural revolution of the '60s, that America is now gone forever. And as one studies the latest projections of the Census Bureau, the America of our grandchildren will be another country altogether, a nation unrecognizable to our parents, a giant Brazil of the North.

In 2050, there will be three times as many people living here as in 1960—420 million. White Americans will be a minority, 49 percent, and falling. Hispanics in the United States, over 100 million, will be equal to the entire population of Mexico today. Our Asian population will be almost as large as our African-American population today.

By countries of origin, America will be a Third World nation. Our cities will look like Los Angeles today. Los Angeles and the cities of Texas, Arizona and California will look like Mexico City.

Eradicating the Border

The ongoing immigration invasion is gradually eradicating the border while creating a Mexican nation within our nation. And the U.S. government, instead of thwarting these developments, is actually encouraging the invasion from the South.

William Norman Grigg, "Stealth Invasion," *New American*, April 5, 2004, p. 14.

What Holds Us Together?

When we all belong to "minorities," what will hold us together? With the rise of group rights and identity pol-

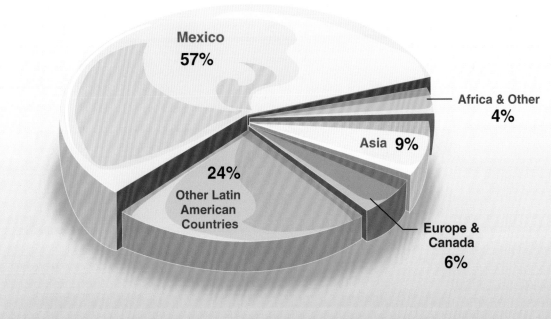

Illegal Immigrants' Countries of Origin

Mexico
57%

Africa & Other
4%

Asia **9%**

24%
Other Latin
American
Countries

Europe &
Canada
6%

Source: Jeffrey Passel, *Unauthorized Migrants: Numbers and Characteristics.* Pew Hispanic Center, Washington D.C., June 14, 2005.

itics, we are already falling out and falling apart over racial preferences and ethnic entitlements.

In the 1990s, for the first time since the Spanish arrived, the white population of California fell. White flight has begun. The white majority, voting with its feet, is ceding the Golden State to Hispanic and Asian immigrants.

Writing in *Foreign Policy*, Harvard Professor Samuel Huntington, author of *Who We Are*, raises an alarm about the huge infusion of Hispanics into the Southwest, and for many reasons.

No Interest in Assimilation

Much of this mass immigration is illegal. Vast numbers are coming here only to work. They are not assimilating. They do not want to become Americans. They are concentrating in states bordering Mexico, which is their country and a nation with a historic grievance against us. They

Some are concerned that children of illegal immigrants will grow up to have a negative view of the United States.

are holding on to their language and culture, creating a Hispanic nation within our nation. By 2050, there will be scores of millions of people living here whose loyalty is to a foreign country.

Moreover, as multiculturalism has captured our schools and colleges, immigrant children will have prejudices and grievances against America and the West reinforced as they learn. The academic elite that controls these schools already paints America as a nation with a rancid history of genocide, slavery, racism, oppression and imperialism.

As immigrant children grow up, who will teach them to love and cherish America? Will they not come to exhibit that same sullen hostility to our country we see erupting at soccer games with Mexico today? There, Mexican fans, whether in the Los Angeles Coliseum or in Guadalajara, curse our players, shout down our national anthem and chant "Osama! Osama!" when the Mexican team scores.

Is the Census Bureau future the future Americans wish? Are they willing to risk it for their grandchildren? No and no are the answers. Why, then, does that future appear inevitable?

Answer: Though a majority of Americans wish to preserve the land they grew up in for their children, our elites—political, academic, cultural and corporate—are either unwilling to conserve that America, or are indifferent to its disappearance, or long for its death.

The Elites Rule

A majority of Americans want immigration cut back and all illegal aliens sent back. Why is the will of the majority, expressed in polls and referenda, not reflected in law or policy? Because we no longer live in a democratic republic. We are ruled by a managerial elite.

America's corporate elites want an endless supply of cheap labor. Our judges throw out popularly enacted laws to which they object. Our academic elites work to see "white, racist America" disappear. Our neo-Marxist cultural elites wish to be the gravediggers of the West and of Christian culture. And America's conservative party, the Republican Party, believes Hispanics hold the key to retention of presidential power, and is desperately anxious not to offend [Mexican president] Vicente Fox.

If, by 2050, the America we grew up in has become a Tower of Babel of squabbling minorities that is falling apart, it will be because of the treason of the elites, and our lack of will to overthrow them.

Analyze the essay:

1. Buchanan starts his essay by describing what life was like in the United States in 1960. Do you believe that he accurately contrasts America in the past with the way it is today?

2. Buchanan concludes that illegal immigration has persisted because it benefits America's elite. Do you agree with this assertion? Why or why not? Use evidence from the text to support your answer.

Illegal Immigrants Embody American Values

Jeff Jacoby

In the following viewpoint Jeff Jacoby asserts that people who enter the United States illegally exhibit values that Americans should admire. According to Jacoby, illegal immigrants risk everything to enter the United States and work hard to pursue the American dream. He believes they desire to learn American culture and positively contribute to the country just as much as legal immigrants and citizens. Jacoby also argues that if immigrants fail to assimilate into American culture, it is not their fault. Instead, the blame should be placed on a politically correct society that does not encourage immigrants to view themselves as Americans.

Jacoby is a columnist for the *Boston Globe*, from which this viewpoint was taken.

Consider the following questions:
1. What proportion of legal immigrants are relatives of people already residing in the United States?
2. According to Jacoby, what type of people do Americans normally admire?
3. What factors have accelerated "the loss of a common English tongue," in the author's view?

Jeff Jacoby, "The Real Cause of the Immigration Crisis," *Boston Globe*, May 21, 2006.
© Copyright 2006 Globe Newspaper Company. Reproduced by permission.

Amid the din over illegal immigration, I have been thinking about two immigrants I happen to know rather well.

Two Immigrants

One is a 3-year-old boy from southern Guatemala. He was brought to the United States in March 2004, one of 11,170 adopted orphans to immigrate that year. The other, who will turn 81 in August, comes from a small village in what is now Slovakia. He entered the United States in the spring of 1948, a few months before his 23rd birthday.

Born an ocean and 78 years apart, these two immigrants might seem on the surface to have little in common. But as naturalized US citizens, they in fact have a great deal in common. English, to mention the most obvious example, is the primary language for both. Neither retains the customs of his native land. Both have a share in the American constitutional patrimony.

The little boy from Guatemala is my younger son. The older man from Slovakia is my father.

Distinguishing Between Legal and Illegal

America is a richer place because my father and son are here, and no doubt most Americans—even those now clamoring for a crackdown on illegal immigration—would agree. Signs reading, "We love legal immigrants," have been on display at rallies organized to

Immigrants catch their first glimpse of the Statue of Liberty as their ship approaches New York Harbor in 1915.

oppose amnesty for illegal immigrants. Another popular sign demands: "What part of illegal don't you understand?"

To countless Americans, the difference between legal and illegal immigration is self-evident and meaningful. But is that really what distinguishes the immigrants we want from those we don't—that the former enter the country lawfully, while the latter break the rules to get here? Are immigrants like my father and son inherently desirable merely because a lot of exasperating bureaucratic requirements were met before they came? Are the 11 million illegal immigrants living within our borders

An immigrant family from Turkey arrives at an airport in Pennsylvania in 2004. Some argue that immigration laws favor those who have American relatives.

unwelcome and problematic only because they got in the wrong way?

Maddening Immigration Laws

A foreigner who enters the United States without first running the immigration-law gantlet is not congenitally unfit to be a good American any more than someone who operates an automobile without a license is congenitally unfit to drive. Our immigration laws are maddening and Byzantine. They are heavily skewed in favor of people related to US citizens—nearly two-thirds of all legal immigrants qualify to enter the United States because they are the relatives of someone already here. If you were designing an immigration system that would admit people on the basis of whether they seemed likely to become good Americans—patriotic, hard working, law-abiding, English-speaking—this is hardly the system you would devise.

Immigrants Embody the American Dream

In so many other contexts, Americans admire self-starters and risk-takers who find ways to get around roadblocks that would defeat less inventive, determined, or gutsy individuals. Of course it is vital, especially after 9/11, to properly control the nation's borders. But there is still something to be said for the self-starters and risk-takers who look at the formidable roadblocks we place in the path of most would-be immigrants, especially those not related to a US citizen—and make up their minds to find a way around them. In his televised remarks [in May 2006], President Bush noted that many illegal aliens "will do anything to come to America to work and build a better life. They walk across miles of desert in the summer heat, or hide in the back of 18-wheelers to reach our country." Aren't those the kind of people America should crave—men and women willing to risk everything, including their lives, for a chance to build their own American dream?

Yes, porous borders are a national-security problem, one too long neglected. But the burning immigration problem of our time isn't that too many people are breaking the rules to get in. It is what they are finding when they get here.

Americans Send a Cynical Message

Instead of a national commitment to assimilation, a cynical multiculturalism sends the message that our culture is no better than any other, so there is no particular reason to embrace the American experience. "Bilingual" education and foreign-language ballots accelerate the loss of a common English tongue, making it easier than ever for newcomers to cluster in linguistic ghettoes. Identity politics erodes the national identity, encouraging immigrants to see themselves first and foremost as members of racial or ethnic groups, and only secondarily as individuals and Americans.

From the day he got off the boat from Europe, my father lived up to the code that expected immigrants to go to work, learn the language, obey the laws, and become an American. My immigrant son, I hope, will live up to it too. The melting pot, it used to be called, before political correctness intervened. That political correctness is what has caused the present crisis. The crisis won't be solved by blaming the immigrants.

Analyze the essay:

1. Jacoby uses his personal experiences to frame this essay. In your opinion do those experiences make his argument more or less compelling? Explain your answer.
2. After reading this viewpoint by Jeff Jacoby and the previous viewpoint by Pat Buchanan, what is your opinion of illegal immigrants' loyalty toward America? Use evidence from this book and other readings to support your argument.

Illegal Immigration Has a Negative Effect on the U.S. Health Care System

Federation for American Immigration Reform

In the following viewpoint the Federation for American Immigration Reform (FAIR) charges that one of the most dangerous effects of illegal immigration is the damage to the U.S. health care system. According to FAIR, contagious diseases that were once rare or nonexistent in the United States, such as typhoid and tuberculosis, are reemerging. The organization further argues that in addition to threatening the health of Americans, illegal immigrants are generally uninsured and thus rely on U.S. taxpayers to pay for their medical care.

FAIR is an organization that works to stop illegal immigration. It believes that the growing flood of immigrants into the United States causes higher unemployment and taxes social services.

Consider the following questions:

1. How much more common is tuberculosis in El Paso County compared to the rest of the United States, as reported by FAIR?
2. As explained by FAIR, how did typhoid reach Maryland in 1992?
3. According to FAIR, what percentage of noncitizens under the age of sixty-five years lack health insurance?

Federation for American Immigration Reform "Illegal Immigration and Public Health," 2005. Reproduced by permission.

The impact of immigration on our public health is often overlooked. Although millions of visitors for tourism and business come every year, the foreign population of special concern is illegal residents, who come most often from countries with endemic health problems and less developed health care. They are of greatest consequence because they are responsible for a disproportionate share of serious public health problems, are living among us for extended periods of time, and often are dependent on U.S. health care services.

Contagious Diseases Are Reemerging

Because illegal immigrants, unlike those who are legally admitted for permanent residence, undergo no medical screening to assure that they are not bearing contagious diseases, the rapidly swelling population of illegal aliens in our country has also set off a resurgence of contagious

Illegal immigrants walk through the village of Sasabe, Mexico, toward the U.S.-Mexico border.

Tuberculosis has been brought to some U.S. schools by foreign students who come from countries where such diseases have not been eradicated.

diseases that had been totally or nearly eradicated by our public health system.

According to Dr. Laurence Nickey, director of the El Paso health district, "Contagious diseases that are generally considered to have been controlled in the United States are readily evident along the border. . . . The incidence of tuberculosis in El Paso County is twice that of the U.S. rate." Dr. Nickey also states that leprosy, which is considered by most Americans to be a disease of the Third World, "is readily evident along the U.S.-Mexico border and that dysentery is several times the U.S. rate. . . . People have come to the border for economic opportunities, but the necessary sewage treatment facilities, public water systems, environmental enforcement, and medical care have not been made available to them, causing a severe risk to health and well being of people on both sides of the border."

"The pork tapeworm, which thrives in Latin America and Mexico, is showing up along the U.S. border, threatening to ravage victims with symptoms ranging from seizures to death. . . . The same [Mexican] underclass has migrated north to find jobs on the border, bringing the parasite and the sickness—cysticercosis—its eggs can cause[.] Cysts that form around the larvae usually lodge in the brain and destroy tissue, causing hallucinations, speech and vision problems, severe headaches, strokes, epileptic seizures, and in rare cases death."

Diseases Beyond the Border

The problem, however, is not confined to the border region, as illegal immigrants have rapidly spread across the country into many new economic sectors such as food processing, construction, and hospitality services.

Typhoid struck Silver Spring, Maryland, in 1992 when an immigrant from the Third World (who had been working in food service in the United States for almost two years) transmitted the bacteria through food at the McDonald's where she worked. River blindness, malaria, and guinea worm, have all been brought to Northern Virginia by immigration.

By default, we grant health passes to illegal aliens. Yet many illegal aliens harbor fatal diseases that American medicine fought and vanquished long ago, such as drug-resistant tuberculosis, malaria, leprosy, plague, polio, dengue, and Chagas disease.

What is unseen is their [illegal aliens'] free medical care that has degraded and closed some of America's finest emergency medical

New Diseases in the United States

[Seven thousand] cases of leprosy have appeared brought in by illegal aliens from India, Brazil, the Caribbean, and Mexico. West Nile virus, which comes from Africa, was unheard of in the United States prior to 1998 and now infects tens of thousands of people in 21 states.

Phyllis Schlafly Report, "Conservative Agenda for 2005: Stop Entry of Illegal Aliens," January 2005, p. 2.

facilities, and caused hospital bankruptcies: 84 California hospitals are closing their doors.[1]

Contrary to common belief, tuberculosis (TB) has not been wiped out in the United States, mostly due to illegal migration. In 1995, there was an outbreak of TB in an Alexandria [Virginia] high school, when 36 high-school students caught the disease from a foreign student. The four greatest immigrant magnet states have over half the TB cases in the U.S. In 1992, 27 percent of the TB cases in the United States were among the foreign-born; in California, it was 61 percent of the cases; in Hawaii, 83 percent; and in Washington state, 46 percent. The Queens, New York, health department attributed 81 percent of new TB cases in 2001 to immigrants.

Costs to U.S. Taxpayers

Immigrants are often uninsured and underinsured. Forty-three percent of noncitizens under 65 have no health insurance. That means there are 9.4 million uninsured immigrants, a majority of whom are in the country illegally, constituting 15 percent of the total uninsured in the nation in the mid-1990s. The cost of the medical care of these uninsured immigrants is passed onto the taxpayer, and strains the financial stability of the health care community.

Another problem is immigrants' use of hospital and emergency services rather than preventative medical care. For example, utilization rate of hospitals and clinics by illegal aliens (29 percent) is more than twice the rate of the overall U.S. population (11 percent).

As a result, the costs of medical care for immigrants are staggering. The estimated cost of unreimbursed medical care in 2004 in California was about $1.4 billion per year. In Texas, the estimated cost was about $.85 billion,

1. Madeleine Peiner Cosman, Ph.D., Esq. "Illegal Aliens and American Medicine," *Journal of American Physicians and Surgeons*, Spring 2005.

Babies born to illegal immigrants cost U.S. taxpayers millions of dollars per year.

and in Arizona the comparable estimate was $.4 billion per year.

One of the frequent costs to U.S. taxpayers is delivery of babies to illegal alien mothers. A California study put the number of these anchor baby deliveries in the state in 1994 at 74,987, at a cost of $215 million. At that time, those births constituted 36 percent of all Medi-Cal births, and they have grown now to substantially more than half or the annual Medi-Cal budget. In 2003, 70 percent of the 2,300 babies born in San Joaquin General Hospital's maternity ward were anchor babies. Medi-Cal in 2003 had 760,000 illegal alien beneficiaries, up from 2002, when there were 470,000.

Analyze the essay:

1. What types of experts were quoted in this essay? What made them qualified to speak on this topic?

2. Throughout this essay FAIR notes that the number of cases of diseases such as tuberculosis has increased, but they do not provide exact numbers. Do you believe their argument would be strengthened if they provided more data? Why do you think FAIR might have excluded this information?

Illegal Immigration Does Not Have a Negative Effect on the U.S. Health Care System

Richard J. Gonzales

Illegal immigrants have been unfairly blamed for high health care costs in the United States, Richard J. Gonzales maintains in the following viewpoint. According to Gonzales, immigrants represent only a small percentage of U.S. health care expenses and use emergency rooms less frequently than citizens do. He further states that immigrants have difficulty gaining access to health care and are often unable to receive treatment outside emergency rooms. He argues that the rising cost of health care is the result of malpractice awards and managed care, not uninsured illegal immigrants.

Gonzales is a columnist for the *Fort Worth Star-Telegram*, from which this viewpoint was taken.

Consider the following questions:

1. According to the Federation of American Immigration Reform report cited by Gonzales, what percentage of immigrants live below the poverty line?
2. According to the study that was published in *American Journal of Public Health*, what was the average health care expense for immigrants in 1998?
3. What does Gonzales say are barriers to immigrant health care access?

The congressional debate over immigration reform is a war of numbers.

If there were a thousand illegal immigrants, little time would be devoted to the issue. However, an estimated 11 million people live, work, play and die in this country without permission from the government.

The Health Care Argument

According to the Federation for American Immigration Reform, more than 1 million illegal immigrants enter the country each year. While here, they earn money—but they also consume expensive health care services. A standard argument by conservative, get-tough-on-the-immigrants organizations such as FAIR is that illegal immigrants are bankrupting our health care system.

According to the group's report, "The Sinking Lifeboat, Uncontrolled Immigration & the U.S. Health Care System":

Some argue that managed care and malpractice settlements, rather than the treatment of illegal immigrants, has raised the cost of health care.

- Thirty-three percent of immigrants have no insurance.
- Sixty-seven percent of counties responding to a survey claim that immigrants are the predominant users of uncompensated health care.
- Sixteen percent of all immigrants live below the poverty line.
- Among full-time wage earners, 51 percent of immigrants have employment-based coverage.
- Communities with high rates of uninsured residents are more likely to reduce hospital services and divert tax dollars to pay for uncompensated care.

Immigrants Receive Less Health Care

Although many immigrants pay Medicare payroll and other taxes, they receive less than half as much health care as native-born families. Immigrant children, in particular, receive 74 percent less health care than U.S.-born children.

Cox News Service, "Immigrants Do Not Burden U.S. Health Care, Study Says," July 26, 2005.

Denying Outpatient Treatment to Immigrants

FAIR expects any immigration reform coming out of Washington to include some plan to reimburse the states and counties for uncompensated immigrant care.

"At a time when the country is struggling to provide affordable care to millions of uninsured residents, President Bush's immigration proposal would bring in hundreds of thousands more uninsured—and officially sanction a massive illegal population already here and already draining health care funds from struggling communities," FAIR says.

For now, hospitals such as John Peter Smith in Fort Worth and Parkland Memorial in Dallas are left holding the doctor's bag.

The JPS board has decided to deny outpatient treatment to illegal immigrants in an effort to save money.

The Allied Communities of Tarrant, a grassroots organization advocating for immigrant health care, has argued that preventive care is less expensive than emergency treatment, so it would make more financial sense to provide outpatient care to all and avoid the high costs that

Health Care Services for Citizens and Immigrants

Immigrants receive about half the health care services provided to native-born Americans.

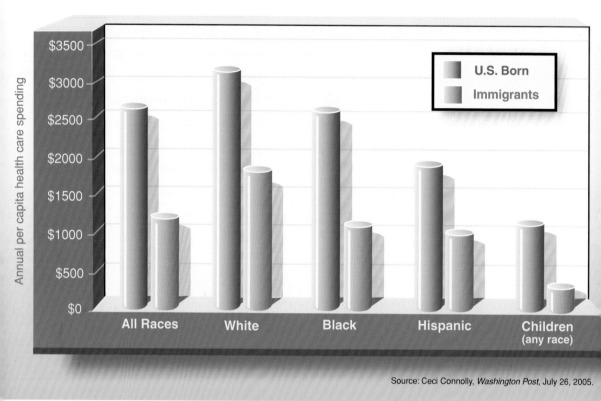

Source: Ceci Connolly, *Washington Post*, July 26, 2005.

come with catastrophic and emergency room care. A majority of the hospital board is unconvinced of any substantial savings.

Costs Have Been Exaggerated

However, this skirts the main issue: the alleged runaway immigrant health care costs.

A study published by six physician-researchers in the August [2005] issue of the *American Journal of Public Health* directly addresses the question of immigrant health care costs compared with citizens' health care costs.

Their study of an analysis of 1998 national survey data of health care expenses differs from FAIR's assessment of who's driving U.S. hospitals to the poorhouse.

According to the physicians, in 1998:

- Immigrant health-care costs were $39.5 billion, or 7.9 percent of the total U.S. health care costs.
- Average health care expenses were $1,139 per immigrant and $2,546 per citizen.
- Uninsured immigrants' expenses were 61 percent lower than those of uninsured U.S. citizens.
- Immigrants younger than 65 had 30 to 75 percent lower expenses than citizens of the same age.
- Immigrant children used the emergency room less often than citizen children, but immigrant children's ER costs were higher.
- Immigrant children in the ER are sicker than citizen children.

Hospital volunteers provide language and cultural aid to elderly Hong Kong immigrants to help them adjust to life in the United States.

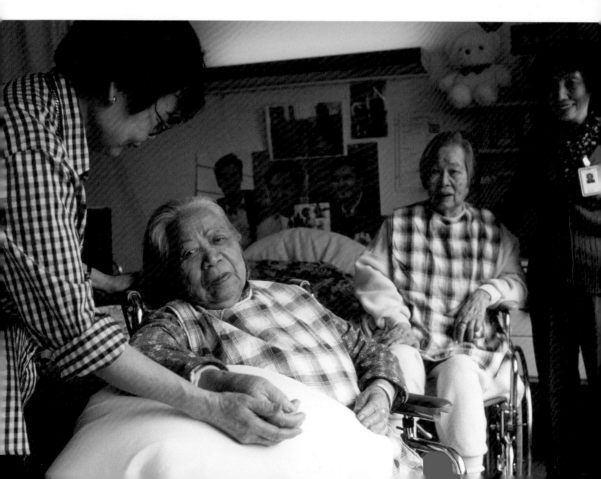

The six physicians conclude that "the deficit of care among immigrants is probably not because of less need; immigrants in our study had slightly worse self-reported health than U.S.-born persons."

Illegal Immigrants Are Unfairly Blamed

Cultural and linguistic factors and fear of deportation have acted as steep barriers to immigrant health care access.

FAIR's assessment of the immigrants' lack of insurance and their low income is accurate. However, to conclude that the immigrants are primarily responsible for uncompensated health care costs is false. The six physicians find no relationship between a state's uncompensated expenses and the percentage of immigrants. They add that policies to terminate publicly sponsored health care coverage will result in little savings.

Based on this research, there is no valid reason to use the immigrant as the whipping boy for spiraling health care expenses. U.S. health care costs are driven by a combination of economic and social forces, such as technology development, drug costs, malpractice awards, managed care, an aging population, lack of disease management, administrative costs and third-party payments.

It's easy to blame the illegal immigrant for high health costs. It's also grossly unfair.

Analyze the essay:

1. In this viewpoint Gonzales compares the results of two studies on immigrants and health care costs. Do you think this comparison made his argument more balanced? Why or why not?
2. How do you think Gonzales might have expanded his argument about what he perceives as the true causes of rising health care costs? Explain your answer.

Section Two:
Model Essays
and Writing
Exercises

The Five-Paragraph Essay

An essay is a short piece of writing that discusses or analyzes one topic. The five-paragraph essay is a form commonly used in school assignments and tests. Every five-paragraph essay begins with an introduction, ends with a conclusion, and features three supporting paragraphs in the middle.

The Thesis Statement. The introduction includes the essay's thesis statement. The thesis statement presents the argument or point the author is trying to make about the topic. The essays in this book all have different thesis statements because they are making different arguments about illegal immigration.

The thesis statement should clearly tell the reader what the essay will be about. A focused thesis statement helps determine what will be in the essay; the subsequent paragraphs are spent developing and supporting its argument.

The Introduction. In addition to presenting the thesis statement, a well-written introductory paragraph captures the attention of the reader and explains why the topic being explored is important. It may provide the reader with background information on the subject matter or feature an anecdote that illustrates a point relevant to the topic. It could also present startling information that clarifies the point of the essay or put forth a contradictory position that the essay will refute. Further techniques for writing an introduction are found later in this section.

Supporting Paragraphs. The introduction is followed by three (or more) supporting paragraphs. These are the main body of the essay. Each paragraph presents and develops a subtopic that supports the essay's thesis statement.

Each subtopic is then supported with its own facts, details, and examples. The writer can use various kinds of supporting material and details to back up the topic of each supporting paragraph. These may include statistics, quotations from people with special knowledge or expertise, historic facts, and anecdotes. A rule of writing is that specific and concrete examples are more convincing than vague, general, or unsupported assertions.

Conclusion. The conclusion is the paragraph that closes the essay. Its function is to summarize or reiterate the main idea of the essay. It may recall an idea from the introduction or briefly examine the larger implications of the thesis. Because the conclusion is also the last chance a writer has to make an impression on the reader, it is important that it not simply repeat what has been presented elsewhere in the essay but close it in a clear, final and memorable way.

   Although the order of the essay's component paragraphs is important, they do not have to be written in that order. Some writers like to decide on a thesis and write the introduction paragraph first. Other writers like to focus first on the body of the essay and write the introduction and conclusion later.

Pitfalls to Avoid

When writing essays about controversial issues such as illegal immigration, it is important to remember that disputes over the material are common precisely because there are many different perspectives. Remember to state your arguments in careful and measured terms. Evaluate your topic fairly—avoid overstating negative qualities of one perspective or understating positive qualities of another. Use examples, facts, and details to support any assertions you make.

Preface B: The Cause-and-Effect Essay

The previous section of this book provides samples of published persuasive writing on illegal immigration. All are persuasive, or opinion, essays making certain arguments about illegal immigration. They are also either cause-and-effect essays or use cause-and-effect reasoning. This section will focus on writing your own cause-and-effect essays.

Cause and effect is a common method of organizing and explaining ideas and events. Simply put, cause and effect is a relationship between two things in which one thing makes something else happen. The *cause* is the reason why something happens. The *effect* is what happens as a result.

A simple example would be a car not starting because it is out of gas. The lack of gas is the cause; the failure to start is the effect. Another example of cause-and-effect reasoning is found in Viewpoint Five. The Federation for American Immigration Reform describes how the influx of uninsured illegal immigrants has led to higher health care costs for U.S. taxpayers. The entrance of illegal immigrants without health insurance is the cause; increased health care costs for taxpayers is the effect.

Not all cause-and-effect relationships are as clear-cut as these two examples. It can be difficult to determine the cause of an effect, especially when talking about society-wide causes and effects. For example, cancer and smoking tobacco have been long associated with each other, but not all cancer patients smoke, and not all smokers get cancer. It took decades of debate and research before the U.S. Surgeon General concluded in 1964 that smoking cigarettes caused cancer (and even then, that conclusion was disputed by tobacco companies for many years thereafter). In Viewpoint One, Steven Camarota writes that illegal immigrants take jobs from native-born Americans. His argument is that illegal immigration is a cause; the loss in jobs an effect. Whether a decrease in job opportunities for native-born Americans can be directly attributable to illegal immigration, or is the effect of other causes, continues to be a matter of debate. Creating and evaluating cause and effect involves both collecting evidence and exercising critical thinking.

Types of Cause-and-Effect Essays

In general, there are three types of cause-and-effect essays. In one type, many causes can contribute to a single effect. Supporting paragraphs would each examine one specific cause. For example, Pat Buchanan in Viewpoint Three argues that by 2050 America will became a completely different country, one that is populated by minorities who have no interest in American values. The causes Buchanan describes include immigrants from Mexico who retain their original language and culture, schools that teach multiculturalism and hatred for America, and corporations that want cheap labor. The ultimate effect of these multiple factors is the possibility that America will become a collection of minorities that have nothing in common.

Another type of cause-and-effect essay examines multiple effects from a single cause. The thesis posits that one event or circumstance has multiple results. An example from this volume is found in Viewpoint Five by the Federation for American Immigration Reform. The organization argues that illegal immigration has had negative effects on health care in the United States, such as an increase in typhoid and tuberculosis, higher health care costs for taxpayers, and the closure of hospitals that cannot afford to provide free health care for illegal immigrants.

A final type of cause-and-effect essay is one that examines a series of causes and effects—a chain of events —in which each link is both the effect of what happened before and the cause of what happens next. Adam Davidson in Viewpoint Two provides one example. Illegal immigrants take jobs, but their presence in the United States creates new jobs for Americans to fill.

Tips to Remember

In writing argumentative essays about controversial issues such as illegal immigration, it is important to remember disputes over cause-and-effect relationships are part of the controversy. Illegal immigration is a complex phenomenon that has multiple effects and multiple causes, and often there is disagreement over what causes what. One needs to be careful and measured in how arguments are expressed. Avoid overstating cause-and-effect relationships if they are unwarranted.

Another pitfall to avoid in writing cause-and-effect essays is to mistake chronology for causation. Just because event X came before event Y does not necessarily mean that X caused Y. Additional evidence may be needed, such as documented studies or similar testimony from many people. Likewise, correlation does not necessarily imply causation. Just because two events happened at the same time does not necessarily mean they are causally related. Again, additional evidence is needed to verify the cause/effect argument.

In the following section you will read some model essays on illegal immigration that use cause-and-effect arguments and do exercises that will help you write your own.

Words and Phrases Common in Cause-and-Effect Essays

accordingly	it then follows that
as a result of	since
because	so
consequently	so that
due to	subsequently
for	therefore
for this reason	this is how
if . . . then	thus

What Causes Illegal Immigration?

Editor's Notes   The following essay is structured as a five-paragraph "multiple cause, single effect" essay. It examines the multiple causes of illegal immigration into the United States. The three causes of illegal immigration are each explored in separate paragraphs. Each of these paragraphs contains supporting details and information, some of which was taken from the viewpoints in the previous section. The essay concludes with a paragraph that restates the essay's main idea: that there are multiple reasons why people enter the United States illegally.

As you read this essay, pay attention to its components and how they are organized (the sidebar notes provide further information on the essay's organization). Also note that all sources are cited using Modern Language Association (MLA) style. For more information on how to cite your sources, see Appendix C.* In addition, consider the following questions:

1. How does the introduction grab the reader's attention?
2. What pieces of supporting evidence are used to back up the essay's arguments?
3. How are quotations used in the essay?

Refers to thesis and topic sentences

Refers to supporting details

Paragraph 1

The problem of illegal immigration is an increasingly discussed issue in American classrooms, businesses, and government institutions. Though there is great debate over the effects illegal immigrants have on the United States—such as whether they drain resources, take jobs from American workers, or dilute American culture—experts on both sides agree that illegal immigration in itself is a growing problem. But before the problem of

*In applying MLA style, the following simplifications have been made: Parenthetical text citations are confined to direct quotations only; electronic source documentation in the Works Cited list omits page ranges and some detailed facts of publication.

illegal immigration can be solved, it seems imperative to explore what causes people to immigrate illegally. There are three main causes of illegal immigration into the United States: restrictive quotas, the visa lottery system, and the search for the American dream. Understanding each of these can give us greater insight into the problem of illegal immigration and better devise systems to solve it.

Paragraph 2

In a sense, the main reason why people illegally immigrate to the United States is very simple. They do it because it is very difficult to enter legally. In addition to an extremely time-consuming application process, there are quotas in place that limit the number of people who are allowed into the country each year. Even though the Immigration Act of 1990 increased the total number of immigrants allowed into the United States each year to 700,000, there are far more people who would like to come to America than the Act would allow. For example, Mexicans and other Central Americans alone are coming to the United States at a rate of more than 500,000 per year (Lowenstein 39). In addition, if you are not already related to a U.S. citizen, it is much harder to become one—according to author Jeff Jacoby, who writes frequently about immigration issues, nearly two-thirds of all legal immigrants who enter the United States are qualified to do so because they are the relatives of someone already here. Thus, people are motivated to immigrate illegally because it is too difficult to do so legally. Some experts believe that these restrictive immigration laws are flawed because, being based on demographics and nepotism, they overlook people who may make excellent citizens. As one writer has put it, "Our immigration laws are maddening and Byzantine [outdated]. . . . If you were designing an immigration system that would admit people on the basis of whether they seemed likely to become good Americans—patriotic, hard working, law-abiding, English-speaking—this is hardly the system you would devise," (Jacoby).

Paragraph 3

Another feature of the United States' immigration system that results in illegal immigration is the visa lottery system. Under this method, people seeking citizenship send in a postcard to the immigration department. Names are drawn out of a hat, and about fifty thousand winners each year are given permanent residence in the United States. Unlike the rules of other immigration protocols, the winners do not need to have a family member already in the United States, possess a particular job skill that is needed, or be fleeing a humanitarian disaster. All they need is the desire to live legally in the United States. However, of all the people who apply for a green card through the visa lottery, only a small percentage actually receives one. For this reason, Steven Camarota, the director of research for the Center for Immigration Studies, believes that this lottery system actually encourages illegal immigration by giving people a sense of false hope that they may someday get chosen to receive a visa. "The lottery's very existence," testified Camarota before the House of Representatives, "tells hundreds of thousands of other people living here illegally, who have no realistic means of ever getting a green card, that they should not go home because one day they too may win the visa lottery, if they play it long enough."

This is the topic sentence of paragraph 3.

Always quote from authoritative sources who are qualified to speak on your topic.

Paragraph 4

Finally, many illegal immigrants are drawn to the United States for the same reasons that legal ones are: to seek good fortune in the land of opportunity. The American dream beckons to people struggling in other countries who see the United States as a place where they can earn more money and live more comfortably. Indeed, the potential for opportunity is enormous. According to the Center for Immigration Studies, the typical Mexican worker earns just one-tenth of what his American counterpart earns: With the opportunity to earn ten times as much money in the United States, it is not hard to understand why many foreigners from poor countries are tempted to

Phrases like "finally" and "indeed" are transitional phrases that help the author move fluidly from one idea to the next.

bypass time-consuming, frustrating immigration laws and enter the country by whatever means possible. Other people enter the country illegally because they are fleeing dangerous, life-threatening situations in their home country and cannot wait to be processed legally. Despite these sad situations, it seems unfair that while many hopeful immigrants pay their dues by waiting the months, even years, for their documents to be processed for legal entry into the country, others cut to the front of the line to illegally take advantage of America's vast opportunities.

The author expresses an opinion in this sentence. How can you tell?

Paragraph 5

These are just a few of the reasons foreigners decide to illegally immigrate to the United States. A better understanding of what motivates people to illegally enter the country can inform the solutions devised for solving the illegal immigration problem. For example, if the visa lottery system encourages illegal immigrants to hang around in the hope they will get selected, perhaps it should be replaced with a system that encourages people to wait in their home countries for U.S. citizenship acceptance. Or, in order to reduce the temptation for foreign workers to seek jobs in the United States, perhaps American business owners should be discouraged from hiring anyone who cannot legally prove he or she is an American citizen. In any case, solving the problem of illegal immigration is a very complicated endeavor that will take the best minds of our country—and perhaps those of other countries—to truly resolve.

The author uses the concluding paragraph to wrap up her ideas and offer suggestions for improving the problem.

Works Cited

Camarota, Steven. "What's Wrong with the Visa Lottery?" Testimony before the U.S. House of Representatives Committee on the Judiciary, Subcommittee on Immigration, Border Security, and Claims, 29 April 2004.

Jacoby, Jeff. "The Real Cause of the Immigration Crisis." *Boston Globe* 21 May 2006.

Lowenstein, Roger. "The Immigration Equation." *New York Times Magazine* 9 July 2006: 36–43, 69–71.

Exercise A: Create an Outline from an Existing Essay

It often helps to create an outline of the five-paragraph essay before you write it. The outline can help you organize the information, arguments, quotes, and evidence you have gathered in your research.

For this exercise, create an outline that could have been used to write Essay One, "What Causes Illegal Immigration?" This "reverse engineering" exercise is meant to help you become familiar with using outlines to classify and arrange information.

To do this you will need to articulate the essay's thesis, identify important pieces of evidence, and point out key comparisons that support the argument. Part of the outline has already been started to give you an idea of the assignment.

Outline

Write the essay's thesis:

I. Supporting Paragraph 1: People illegally immigrate to the United States because it is very difficult to enter legally.

A.

B. Preference given to those with family members already inside the United States.

II. Supporting Paragraph 2:

A.

B. Quote from Steven Camarota

III. Supporting Paragraph 3: Illegal immigrants are drawn to the United States for the same reasons that legal ones are: to seek good fortune in the land of opportunity.

A.

B.

Illegal Immigration: Criminalizing America

Editor's Notes This model essay is structured as a five-paragraph "one cause, multiple effects" cause-and-effect essay. It argues that illegal immigration has multiple effects on crime in America. Each of the three supporting paragraphs details one effect illegal immigrants have on crime. In the first supporting paragraph the writer argues that murder, drug trafficking, and other crimes are frequently perpetrated by illegal immigrants. The second supporting paragraph looks at the spread of a gang dominated by illegal aliens. In the third supporting paragraph the writer explains the economic effects of crimes committed by illegal immigrants. The writer concludes with a paragraph that summarizes the arguments made in the essay and reiterates the essay's main idea: that illegal immigrants cause crime.

Unlike the first model essay, the second model essay supports a particular point of view about illegal immigration. In this way, it is a persuasive essay; it attempts to persuade the reader of a particular point of view. As you read the essay, consider the points raised and sources cited. The questions in the margins will help you further understand the essay's structure and how it is organized.

Paragraph 1

The essay opens with an anecdote that describes a violent crime spree committed by an illegal immigrant. It is intended to grab the reader's attention.

During the late summer and early fall of 2002, a sniper struck the greater Washington, D.C., area. Residents were terrified of being gunned down as they ran errands or filled their cars with gas. Before the horror ended, ten people were killed and three injured during the random attacks. Two men were arrested: John Allen Muhammad and Lee Boyd Malvo. As it turns out, Malvo had entered the United States illegally. Malvo is one of the estimated 11 million to 20 million illegal immigrants who reside in the United

States. America's immigration laws are not the only rules these residents break. One of the most serious effects of illegal immigration is crime against American citizens.

Paragraph 2

Illegal aliens commit a variety of crimes, including murder, drug trafficking, and property destruction. According to a report by the Urban Institute, a think tank that deals with social issues such as immigration, the major offenses for which illegal aliens are convicted in federal court include entering the United States unlawfully, drug trafficking, murder, and fraud (Clark and Anderson 4). William Norman Grigg, senior editor of *New American*, confirms this problem, writing that "one out of every four homicides in Colorado is committed by an illegal alien who flees to Mexico." Grigg also cites a study published in the *Journal of American Physicians and Surgeons* that found that a whopping 95 percent of outstanding homicide warrants in Los Angeles County are for illegal aliens. Clearly, illegal immigrants do not end their rule-breaking at the nation's immigration laws. Their disrespect for our nation's laws puts native-born citizens in unnecessary danger.

Paragraph 3

In addition to homicide, carjacking, and property destruction, illegal immigrants also contribute to gang activity. In fact, one of the nation's most powerful gangs is dominated by illegal aliens and has spread to thirty-three states. Founded in El Salvador and known as MS-13 (an abbreviation of Mara Salvatrucha, which roughly translates to "a posse of street-tough Salvadorans"), its members have been linked to murder, gang rapes, and drug smuggling. According to an article published in *Newsweek* by author Ariana Campo-Flores, between eight thousand and ten thousand people belong to MS-13's American gangs. The size of MS-13 and its presence in so many states makes it difficult for law enforcement to successfully stem the problem. As Campo-Flores explains, "While machete attacks might occur on the East Coast, they're

What is the essay's thesis statement?

What is the topic sentence for paragraph 2?

What sources are cited throughout the essay to lend authority to the points and claims?

The author expresses an opinion in this sentence. How can you tell?

What transitional phrases are used to keep the ideas in the essay moving?

rare on the West Coast. While car thefts and drug trafficking might be big in North Carolina, gang-on-gang violence predominates in Virginia. It's that decentralized nature of MS-13—with no clear hierarchy or structure—that makes it so vexing to authorities."

Paragraph 4

What is the topic sentence of paragraph 4?

The effects illegal immigration has on crime in the United States do not cease even if the offenders are arrested. Because of the substantial economic cost of putting illegal immigrants through the U.S. criminal justice system, even when illegals are arrested they continue to cost American taxpayers. The Bureau of Prisons has reported that more than 30 percent of inmates were born outside the United States. A study conducted by the University of Arizona found that the cost to arrest, prosecute, and jail illegal immigrants in the twenty-eight counties bordering the U.S.-Mexico border totals $125 million per year. Colorado alone was reimbursed a total of $5.7 million in 2004 by the federal government for the costs of incarcerating illegal aliens (Colorado Alliance for Immigration Reform). For the border states as a whole, the total reaches more than $1 billion.

Paragraph 5

The concluding paragraph refers back to the opening of the essay.

The essay closes by reiterating its main argument. After reading the essay, do you agree with the author?

Lee Boyd Malvo's role in the shooting spree is one of the more famous examples of the danger that criminal illegal immigrants pose to Americans. Critics of illegal immigration point out that these crimes are not limited to the states closest to the border and that Americans throughout the United States are at risk of becoming victims. While immigration can have numerous positive effects, such as introducing new cultures and ideas, it can also prove socially and economically costly to native-born residents.

Works Cited

Campo-Flores, Ariana. "The Most Dangerous Gang in America," *Newsweek* 28 Mar. 2006.

Clark, Rebecca, and Scott A. Anderson. "Illegal Aliens in Federal, State and Local Criminal Justice Systems." Urban Institute. 30 June 2000. www.urban.org/publications/410366.html

"Crime and Illegal Aliens in Colorado." Colorado Alliance for Immigration Reform. 19 May 2006. www.cairco.org/issues/issues_crime_colorado.html.

Grigg, William Norman. "The Bloody Border," *New American* 13 June 2006.

Exercise A: Create an Outline from an Existing Essay

As you did for the first model essay in this section, create an outline that could have been used to write "Illegal Immigration: Criminalizing America." Be sure to identify the essay's thesis statement, its supporting ideas, its descriptive passages, and key pieces of evidence that are used.

The second model essay presents one point of view regarding illegal immigration. For this exercise, your assignment is to find supporting ideas, choose specific and concrete details, create an outline, and ultimately write a five-paragraph essay that argues an opposing view. (A later assignment in this book will ask you to practice writing the introduction and conclusion for this essay.)

Step 1. Find supporting ideas.

You may use information found in Sections One and Three of this book as well as do outside research on your topic.

   a. After researching, write down three or more arguments that support the following thesis statement: Illegal Immigrants Positively Contribute to Society. Your goal is to find three different positive effects that illegal immigrants have on American society. Each effect becomes the subject of a paragraph and should be expressed in the paragraph's topic sentence. Example: "Illegal immigrants help American society function by doing jobs that need to get done but that citizens do not want to do."

   Supporting evidence might include this quote from Adam Davidson in Viewpoint Two:

   > Illegal immigrants do often take some of the country's least attractive jobs, such as in meat packing and agriculture. If there were no undocumented workers available for those jobs, employers would likely invest in new technology, replacing workers with automation.

   b. Choose two other arguments that can become paragraph topics. For each cause, write down facts or information that support it. These could include any of the following types of information:

- statistical data
- research findings and conclusions
- quotes from articles or Web sites
- anecdotes of past events

Step 2. Place the information from Step 1 in outline form.

Step 3. Write the arguments or supporting statements in paragraph form.

You now have three arguments that support the essay's thesis statement. Use the outline to write out your three supporting arguments in paragraph form. Make sure each paragraph has a topic sentence that states the paragraph's topic clearly and broadly. Then, add supporting sentences that express the facts, quotes, details, and examples that support the paragraph's argument. The paragraph may also have a concluding or summary sentence.

Imagining Amnesty for Illegal Immigrants: A Bad Solution to a Growing Problem

Editor's Notes So far you have seen examples of a multiple-effect essay and a multiple-cause essay. The following piece is an example of a third type of cause-and-effect essay: a chain-of-events essay. Instead of arguing that factors A, B, and C caused phenomenon X, this piece argues that A caused B, which in turn caused C, which in turn caused X. This is sometimes known as the domino effect. Chronology—the order of events—plays an important part in this type of essay.

This essay focuses on what would happen if all illegal immigrants in the United States were granted amnesty or were allowed to become legal residents. Each paragraph details a different link in the chain of what might happen if amnesty was granted to illegal immigrants.

This essay also differs from the first two model essays in that it is longer than five paragraphs. Many ideas require more paragraphs for adequate development. Moreover, the ability to write a sustained research or position paper is a valuable skill. Learning how to develop a longer piece of writing gives you the tools you will need to advance academically.

As you read the essay, consider the questions posed in the notes in the margin. They will help you understand how the essay is organized.

■ Refers to thesis and topic sentences

■ Refers to supporting details

Paragraph 1

Illegal immigration has long been a problem for the United States, and there are heated debates over how to solve this growing problem. One recent solution put forth was the Comprehensive Immigration Reform Act (CIRA) of 2006. The Act, known as S.2611, proposed offering amnesty and citizenship to current illegal aliens—that is, to solve the problem of illegal immigration by granting all illegals currently living in the country legal status. By various methods, S.2611 would legalize between 60 and 85 percent of the nation's current 11.9 million illegal immigrants, up to some 9 to 10 million individuals (Rector). But would legalizing such people really solve the problem of illegal immigration? In order to answer that question, it is necessary to consider what would happen if illegal immigrants were to become legalized. Examining this hypothetical chain of events will allow us to see that although there would be some positive outcomes of amnesty programs, overall they are not the solution to America's illegal immigration problem—in fact, they appear likely to make the problem even worse.

What is the essay's thesis statement?

Paragraph 2

What transitional phrases are used to connect the ideas in paragraph 2?

The first thing that would happen if illegal immigrants became legal residents of the United States is that their incomes would likely rise. Currently, illegal immigrants, being illegal, have very few labor rights. They are usually hired to do very low-paying jobs in rough conditions, such as working below the legal minimum wage without breaks or for extreme lengths of time. Because they are working in violation of U.S. law, they have no legal recourse to challenge these conditions or sue their employers for unfair treatment. If they were to become legal, however, this situation would be reversed. It would be illegal to pay them anything less than the minimum wage and they would be entitled to the working conditions dictated by U.S. law.

Paragraph 3

What is the topic sentence for paragraph 3?

However, despite an increase in earnings, millions of newly legalized immigrants would cost the United States millions of additional dollars because they would increase their use of public services. When they are illegal, immigrants are ineligible to benefit from most public programs. But granting citizenship would make millions of new people eligible for welfare programs such as the earned income credit, food stamps, Medicaid, and Temporary Assistance to Needy Families (Rector). Although the newly legalized immigrants would be paying more taxes on their higher incomes, a 2004 Center for Immigration Studies report found that this amount would not be enough to offset the additional costs incurred by their service use. According to the CIS, if ten million illegal immigrants were granted amnesty, the cost of federal benefits and social services to such people would increase by about $8,000 per household, but federal tax payments made by such households would only increase by about $3,000. Put another way, total costs could grow from $10.4 billion a year to almost $29 billion. Taxpayers simply cannot afford to shoulder this expensive and unfair burden.

Paragraph 4

With access to higher income and public services, newly legalized immigrants would next be freer to make decisions about what types of jobs they worked. Currently, illegal immigrants are confined to industries which allow them to be paid under the table or hired on a per-day basis—these typically consist of agriculture or backroom service jobs. But instead of having to hop on the truck of a farmer seeking strawberry pickers for a day, having legal work status would allow people to choose from a variety of different industries that offer them better working conditions and opportunity for advancement. Overall, if illegal immigrants were to become legal residents, they would likely see an increase in pay, an increase in job opportunity, and would be less likely to be exploited by employers.

What transitional phrases are used throughout the essay?

Paragraph 5

Once formerly illegal immigrants begin leaving their jobs to find better, high-paying ones, a huge gap would be left in the lower levels of the American job market. While this could theoretically create the opportunity for other Americans to take these jobs, in reality it would leave

What chain of events
has been chronicled
thus far in the essay?

many undesirable yet important positions open and unfilled. If illegal immigrants did not pick strawberries, wash dishes, or provide nanny or cleaning services, it is unlikely these jobs would be taken by legal Americans. This is because illegal immigrants tend to take jobs Americans do not want to do, rather than taking jobs away from them. As one author writes, "Mexicans [and other illegal immigrants] are supplying a skill level that is much in demand. It doesn't just seem that Americans don't want to be hotel chambermaids, pick lettuce or repair roofs; it's true. . . . [Illegals] perform services that would otherwise be more expensive and in some cases simply unavailable" (Lowenstein 40). Without legal replacements for illegal workers, the very fabric of America's industries could be thrown into a labor shortage crisis.

Paragraph 6

How does the first sen-
tence of the sixth para-
graph show a causal
connection between the
ideas in paragraphs 5
and 6?

With jobs open and few people in America to fill them, new crops of illegal immigrants will likely be encouraged to enter the country to take these jobs. Indeed, the United States has experienced this phenomenon before. In 1986 an act called the Immigration Reform and Control Act (IRCA) granted amnesty to 2.7 million undocumented immigrants who were at the time residing in the country illegally. It was thought that the act would curb illegal immigration by better incorporating this sector of people into society. But in fact, as Robert Rector of the Heritage Foundation notes, "the Act did nothing to stem the tide of illegal entry . . . the prospect of future amnesty and citizenship served as a magnet to draw even more illegal immigrants into the country. After all, if the nation granted amnesty once why wouldn't it do so again?" According to Rector, the number of illegal aliens entering the country dramatically increased

What authorities are
quoted in the essay?

after IRCA went into effect. Indeed, illegal immigration grew from about 140,000 people per year in the 1980s to about 700,000 per year today. The mistake of 1986 surely indicates that granting amnesty only worsens the problem of illegal immigration.

Paragraph 7

The addition of new illegal immigrants and newly legalized ones would lead to a final problem for the United States: It would cause a drastic increase in the nation's population boom, which would have dire consequences for everyone living in the country. In addition to hundreds of thousands of new illegal immigrants who would enter the country each year, newly legalized immigrants would have the right to bring over family members such as spouses, children, and parents from abroad. A 2002 study by an organization called Negative Population Growth (NPG) showed that if five to six million illegal immigrants were given amnesty, an astonishing 30 to 50 million more foreigners could become candidates for immigration—just from being related to those who had been given amnesty! Once in the United States, these people would be eligible to receive social services and government-funded medical care, placing further drain on the nation's resources and burdening taxpayers with the costs. "While no one can predict how many spouses, children, and parents of the beneficiaries of amnesty would enter the country, the pool of those who could enter is enormous, and the potential long-term government costs would be staggering" (Rector). The United States is not in the position to add millions of additional citizens to its ranks—its services, land, and resources would be overrun with people who entered as a by-product of the amnesty program.

What information is used to support the argument of paragraph 7?

Paragraph 8

As this hypothetical chain of events shows, widespread amnesty programs make the problem of illegal immigration worse. The United States should not reward people with citizenship for breaking its immigration laws. Nor should it attempt to define away the problem of illegal immigration by relabeling people. A saner approach to curbing illegal immigration would include tightening border patrol and developing a better system of making employers punishable for hiring illegal labor, just to name

What idea from the introduction does the essay return to?

a few alternatives. Amnesty programs should not be a part of the Comprehensive Immigration Reform Act (CIRA) of 2006 or of any legislation seeking to truly reduce the problem of illegal immigration in America.

Works Cited

"The High Cost of Cheap Labor: Illegal Immigration and the Federal Budget." Center for Immigration Studies. 25 Aug. 2004. www.cis.org/articles/2004/fiscal.html.

Lowenstein, Roger. "The Immigration Equation." *New York Times Magazine* 9 July 2006.

Rector, Robert. "Amnesty and Continued Low Skill Immigration Will Substantially Raise Welfare Costs and Poverty." *Backgrounder #1936*. Heritage Foundation 12 May 2006.

"Zero Tolerance for Illegal Immigration: An Urgent Policy Need." Negative Population Growth, 2006 < www.npg. org/pospapers/zerotolerance.html > .

Exercise A: Examining Introductions and Conclusions

Every essay features introductory and concluding paragraphs that are used to frame the main ideas being presented. Along with presenting the essay's thesis statement, well-written introductions should grab the attention of the reader and make clear why the topic being explored is important. The conclusion reiterates the essay's thesis and is also the last chance for the writer to make an impression on the reader. Strong introductions and conclusions can greatly enhance an essay's effect on an audience.

The Introduction

There are several techniques that can be used to craft an introductory paragraph. An essay can start with

- an anecdote: a brief story that illustrates a point relevant to the topic;
- startling information: facts or statistics that elucidate the point of the essay;
- setting up and knocking down a position: a position or claim believed by proponents of one side of a controversy, followed by statements that challenge that claim;
- historical perspective: an example of the way things used to be that leads into a discussion of how or why things work differently now;
- summary information: general introductory information about the topic that feeds into the essay's thesis statement.

1. Reread the introductory paragraphs of the model essays and of the viewpoints in Section One. Identify which of the techniques described above are used in the example essays. How do they grab the attention of the reader? Are their thesis statements clearly presented?

2. Write an introduction for the essay you have outlined and partially written in the exercise that accompanied Essay Two using one of the techniques described above.

The Conclusion

The conclusion brings the essay to a close by summarizing or returning to its main ideas. Good conclusions, however, go beyond simply repeating these ideas. Strong conclusions explore a topic's broader implications and reiterate why it is important to consider. They may frame the essay by returning to an anecdote featured in the opening paragraph. Or they may close with a quotation or refer back to an event in the essay. In opinionated essays, the conclusion can reiterate which side the essay is taking or ask the reader to reconsider a previously held position on the subject.

1. Reread the concluding paragraphs of the model essays and of the viewpoints in Section One. Which were most effective in driving their arguments home to the reader? What sorts of techniques did they use to do this? Did they appeal emotionally to the reader, or bookend an idea or event referenced elsewhere in the essay?

2. Write a conclusion for the essay you have outlined and partially written in the previous exercise using one of the techniques described above.

Exercise B: Using Quotations to Enliven Your Essay

No essay is complete without quotations. Get in the habit of using quotes to support at least some of the ideas in your essays. Quotes do not need to appear in every paragraph but should appear often enough so that the essay contains voices aside from your own. When you write, use quotations to accomplish the following:

1. Provide expert advice that you are not necessarily in the position to know about
2. Cite lively or passionate passages
3. Include a particularly well-written point that gets to the heart of the matter
4. Supply statistics or facts that have been derived from someone's research
5. Deliver anecdotes that illustrate the point you are trying to make
6. Express first-person testimony

Now reread the essays presented in all sections of this book and find at least one example of each of the above quotation types.

There are a few important things to remember when using quotations:

- Note your sources' qualifications and biases. This way your reader can identify the person you have quoted and can put their words in a context.
- Put any quoted material within proper quotation marks. Failing to attribute quotes to their authors constitutes plagiarism, which is when an author takes someone else's words or ideas and presents them as his or her own. Plagiarism is a very serious infraction and must be avoided at all costs.

Author's Checklist

✔ Review the five-paragraph essay you wrote.
✔ Make sure it has a clear introduction that draws the reader in and contains a thesis statement that concisely expresses what your essay is about.
✔ Evaluate the paragraphs and make sure they each have clear topic sentences that are well supported by interesting and relevant details.
✔ Check that you have used compelling and authoritative quotes to enliven the essay.
✔ Finally, be sure you have a solid conclusion that uses one of the techniques presented in this exercise.

Final Writing Challenge: Write Your Own Five-Paragraph Cause-and-Effect Essay

Using the material in this book, write your own five-paragraph cause-and-effect essay that deals with illegal immigration. The following steps are suggestions on how to get started.

1. Choose your topic.

Think carefully before deciding on the topic of your cause-and-effect essay. Is there any subject that particularly fascinates you? Is there an issue you strongly support or feel strongly against? Is there a topic you would like to learn more about? Ask yourself such questions before selecting your essay topic. Refer to Appendix D: Sample Essay Topics if you need help selecting a topic.

2. Write down questions and answers about the topic.

Before you begin writing, you will need to think carefully about what ideas your essay will contain. This is a process known as *brainstorming*. Brainstorming involves asking yourself questions and coming up with ideas to discuss in your essay. Possible questions that will help you with the brainstorming process include:

- Why is this topic important?
- Why should people be interested in this topic?
- How can I make this essay interesting to the reader?
- What question am I going to address in this paragraph or essay?
- What facts, ideas, or quotes can I use to support the answer to my question?
- Will the question's answer reveal a preference for one subject over another?

Questions especially for cause-and-effect essays include:
- What are the causes of the topic being examined?
- What are the effects of the topic being examined?
- Are there single or multiple causes?

- Are there single or multiple effects?
- Is a chain reaction of events involved?

3. Gather facts and ideas related to your topic.
This book contains several places to find information, including the viewpoints and the appendixes. In addition, you may want to research the books, articles, and Web sites listed in Section Three, or do additional research in your local library.

4. Develop a workable thesis statement.
Use what you have written down in steps 2 and 3 above to help you articulate the main point or argument you want to make in your essay. It should be expressed in a clear sentence and make an arguable or supportable point.

Examples:

Illegal immigration is a drain on government resources.
This could be the thesis statement of a multiple-effect essay that looks at how illegal immigration affects the money the government spends on health care, education, and social services.

.

Illegal immigrants help America function.
This could be the basis of a chain-of-events essay that looks at what might happen if illegal immigrants were simultaneously removed from the country.

5. Write an outline or diagram.
a. Write the thesis statement at the top of the outline.
b. Write roman numerals I, II, and III on the left side of the page with A, B, and C under each numeral.
c. Next to each roman numeral, write down the best ideas you came up with in step 3. These should all directly relate to and support the thesis statement.
d. Next to each letter write down information that supports that particular idea.

6. Write the three supporting paragraphs.

Use your outline to write the three supporting paragraphs. Write down the main idea of each paragraph in sentence form. Do the same thing for the supporting points of information. Each sentence should support the paragraph of the topic. Be sure you have relevant and interesting details, facts, and quotes. Use transitions when you move from idea to idea to keep the text fluid. Sometimes, although not always, paragraphs can include a concluding or summary sentence that restates the paragraph's argument.

7. Write the introduction and conclusion.

See the exercise that accompanies Essay Three for information on writing introductions and conclusions.

8. Read and rewrite.

As you read, check your essay for the following:

- ✔ Does the essay maintain a consistent tone?
- ✔ Do all sentences serve to reinforce your general thesis or your paragraph theses?
- ✔ Do all paragraphs flow from one to the other? Do you need to add transition words or phrases?
- ✔ Have you quoted from reliable, authoritative, and interesting sources?
- ✔ Is there a sense of progression throughout the essay?
- ✔ Does the essay get bogged down in too much detail or irrelevant material?
- ✔ Does your introduction grab the reader's attention?
- ✔ Does your conclusion reflect back on any previously discussed material or give the essay a sense of closure?
- ✔ Are there any spelling or grammatical errors?

Tips on Writing Effective Cause-and-Effect Essays

- You do not need to include every detail on your subjects. Focus on the most important ones that support your thesis statement.
- Vary your sentence structure; avoid repeating yourself.
- Maintain a professional, objective tone of voice. Avoid sounding uncertain or insulting.
- Anticipate what the reader's counter arguments may be and answer them.
- Use sources that state facts and evidence.
- Avoid assumptions or generalizations without evidence.
- Aim for clear, fluid, well-written sentences that together make up an essay that is informative, interesting, and memorable.

Section Three: Supporting Research Material

Facts About Illegal Immigration

Editor's Note: These facts can be used in reports or papers to reinforce or add credibility when making important points or claims.

The Demographics of Illegal Immigration

- According to the Census Bureau, 35 million immigrants lived in the United States in March 2005. Of those, between 9 and 10 million were illegal.
- Immigrants who entered the United States between January 2000 and March 2005 numbered 7.9 million. According to a study by Steven A. Camarota of the Center for Immigration Studies, 3.7 million of these immigrants entered illegally.
- The Census Bureau estimates that due in part to immigration, the U.S. population will reach 400 million before 2055.
- Of the U.S. population, 11.5 percent, or 33.1 million people, were born outside the United States.
- According to the Web site of Minnesota congressman Gil Gutknecht, births to illegal aliens account for one in ten births in the United States.

Economic Statistics

- The Census Bureau reports that one-third of the immigrant population lacks health insurance.
- Based on Census Bureau reports, Camarota estimates that 61 percent of illegal immigrants who are at least twenty-one years old have not completed high school.
- Approximately 6.2 percent of illegal immigrants live in poverty.
- The Federation for American Immigration Reform reports that the average illegal immigrant is thirty-

two years old, earns $8,982 per year, and has received seven years of education.
- A report by the Congressional Research Service found that 55 percent of hired farm workers are not authorized to work in the United States.

The Southern Border
- Of all immigrants to the United States, 31 percent come from Mexico, with 10.8 million living in the United States as of 2005.
- Of all immigrants living in the United States, 54 percent came from Mexico, the Caribbean, and Central and South America; 18 percent arrived from East Asia.
- According to a report by the Center for Immigration Studies, an estimated 68.4 percent of illegal aliens from Mexico lack health insurance.
- The border between the United States and Mexico is 1,940 miles long and is patrolled by 9,539 border patrol agents, according to the *Washington Times*.

The Northern Border
- Three percent of illegal immigrants cross over the U.S.-Canada border, according to the *Detroit News*.
- According to U.S. immigration authorities, between three thousand and five thousand Chinese immigrants enter the United States illegally. Almost all of them arrive through Canada.
- The Bureau of Customs and Border Protection has reported that illegal immigrants from sixty nations, including Afghanistan and Pakistan, attempt to cross the Canadian border every year.
- The border between Canada and the United States is 4,121 miles long. It is guarded by 999 border patrol agents, according to the *Washington Times*.

Public Opinion About Illegal Immigration

- A January 2006 poll conducted by *Time* magazine found that 89 percent of Americans think illegal immigration is a problem.
- According to a December 2005 poll conducted by the *Washington Post* and *ABC News*, 79 percent of Americans believe that the United States is not doing enough to keep illegal immigrants from entering the country.
- A June 2006 Gallup poll found that 66 percent of Americans believe that illegal immigrants cost taxpayers too much by using public services like health care and education.

A Timeline of Actions Taken by the U.S. Government

- The rise in illegal immigration from Mexico into Texas and California prompts the United States to implement Operation Wetback in 1954. Illegal immigrants are rounded up and sent back to Mexico.
- The Immigration and Reform Control Act is signed into law in 1986. The law gives amnesty to all illegal aliens who were living in the United States at that time. It also prohibits employers from knowingly hiring or recruiting illegal immigrants.
- In 1990 the U.S. Congress passed a new version of the Immigration Reform and Control Act (IRCA). As a result of the law, 2.7 million illegal immigrants were given green cards.
- Congress passes the Illegal Immigration Reform and Immigrant Responsibility Act in 1996. The law strengthens border enforcement and makes it more difficult for refugees to gain asylum. In addition, the welfare reform act signed into law that year by President Bill Clinton makes illegal immigrants ineligible for almost all federal and

state benefits, the exceptions being disaster relief, immunization programs, and emergency medical care.

- The Immigration and Naturalization Service (INS) was dissolved in 2003 and its responsibilities transferred to the Department of Homeland Security.

Finding and Using Sources of Information

No matter what type of essay you are writing, it is necessary to find information to support your point of view. You can use sources such as books, magazine articles, newspaper articles, and online articles.

Using Books and Articles

You can find books and articles in a library by using the library's computer or cataloging system. If you are not sure how to use these resources, ask a librarian to help you. You can also use a computer to find many magazine articles and other articles written specifically for the Internet.

You are likely to find a lot more information than you can possibly use in your essay, so your first task is to narrow it down to what is likely to be most usable. Look at book and article titles. Look at book chapter titles, and examine the book's index to see if it contains information on the specific topic you want to write about. (For example, if you want to write about possible connections between illegal immigration and terrorism and you find a book about terrorism, check the chapter titles and index to be sure it contains information about illegal immigration.)

For a five-paragraph essay, you do not need a great deal of supporting information, so quickly try to narrow down your materials to a few good books and magazine or Internet articles. You do not need dozens. You might even find that one or two good books or articles contain all the information you need.

You probably do not have time to read an entire book, so find the chapters or sections that relate to your topic, and skim these. When you find useful information, copy it onto a notecard or notebook. You should look for supporting facts, statistics, quotations, and examples.

Using the Internet

When you select your supporting information, it is important that you evaluate its source. This is especially important with information you find on the Internet. Because nearly anyone can put information on the Internet, there is as much bad information as good information. Before using Internet information—or any information—try to determine if the source seems to be reliable. Is the author or Internet site sponsored by a legitimate organization? Is it from a government source? Does the author have any special knowledge or training relating to the topic you are looking up? Does the article give any indication of where its information comes from?

Using Your Supporting Information

When you use supporting information from a book, article, interview, or other source, there are three important things to remember:

1. Make it clear whether you are using a direct quotation or a paraphrase. If you copy information directly from your source, you are quoting it. You must put quotation marks around the information and tell where the information comes from. If you put the information in your own words, you are paraphrasing it.

Here is an example of a using a quotation:

> Glynn Custred believes that illegal immigration places a heavy toll on U.S. taxpayers. He writes: "Recently, the National Research Council estimated that the total cost to the taxpayer of illegal immigration, which is carried mainly by local and state governments, is $11 to $22 billion a year for education, criminal justice, and medical care," (23).

Here is an example of a brief paraphrase of the same passage:

Author Glynn Custred argues that U.S. taxpayers are burdened by the heavy costs of providing basic services to illegal immigrants. He cites research showing that local and state governments spend between $11 to $22 billion annually on education, medical care, and criminal justice for illegal immigrants.

2. Use the information fairly. Be careful to use supporting information in the way the author intended it. For example, it is unfair to quote an author as saying, "Illegal immigrants take jobs away from Americans" when he or she intended to say, "Illegal immigrants take jobs away from Americans but the blame lies with business owners who want to pay lower wages." This is called taking information out of context. Using that information as supporting evidence is unfair.

3. Give credit where credit is due. Giving credit is known as citing. You must use citations when you use someone else's information, but not every piece of supporting information needs a citation.

   - If the supporting information is general knowledge—that is, it can be found in many sources—you do not have to cite your source.
   - If you directly quote a source, you must cite it.
   - If you paraphrase information from a specific source, you must cite it.

If you do not use citations where you should, you are plagiarizing—or stealing—someone else's work.

Citing Your Sources
There are a number of ways to cite your sources. Your teacher will probably want you to do it in one of three ways:

- Informal: As in the examples in number 1 above, tell where you got the information in the same place you use it.
- Informal list: At the end of the article, place an unnumbered list of the sources you used. This tells the reader where, in general, you got your information.
- Formal: Use a note. An endnote is generally placed at the end of an article or essay, although it may be located in different places depending on your teacher's requirements.

Works Cited

Custred, Glynn. "Where Are My Juice and Crackers?" *American Spectator* July/Aug. 2005.

Using MLA Style to Create a Works-Cited List

You will probably need to create a list of works cited for your paper. These include materials that you quoted from, relied heavily on, or consulted to write your paper. There are several different ways to structure these references. The following examples are based on Modern Language Association (MLA) style, one of the major citation styles used by writers.

Book Entries

For most book entries you will need the author's name, the book's title, where it was published, what company published it, and the year it was published. This information is usually found on the inside of the book. Variations on book entries include the following:

A book by a single author:
Guest, Emma. *Children of AIDS: Africa's Orphan Crisis.* London: Sterling, 2003.

Two or more books by the same author:
Friedman, Thomas L. *From Beirut to Jerusalem.* New York: Doubleday, 1989.
————. *The World Is Flat: A Brief History of the Twentieth Century.* New York: Farrar, Straus and Giroux, 2005.

A book by two or more authors:
Pojman, Louis P., and Jeffrey Reiman. *The Death Penalty: For and Against.* Lanham, MD: Rowman & Littlefield, 1998.

A book with an editor:
Friedman, Lauri S., ed. *At Issue: What Motivates Suicide Bombers?* San Diego: Greenhaven, 2004.

Periodical and Newspaper Entries

Entries for sources found in periodicals and newspapers are cited a bit differently than books. For one, these sources usually have a title and a publication name. They also may have specific dates and page numbers. Unlike book entries, you do not need to list where newspapers or periodicals are published or what company publishes them.

An article from a periodical:
> Snow, Keith Harmon. "State Terror in Ethiopia." *Z Magazine* June 2004: 33–35.

An unsigned article from a periodical:
> "Broadcast Decency Rules." *Issues & Controversies On File* 30 Apr. 2004.

An article from a newspaper:
> Constantino, Rebecca. "Fostering Love, Respecting Race." *Los Angeles Times* 14 Dec. 2002: B17.

Internet Sources

To document a source you found online, try to provide as much information on it as possible, including the author's name, the title of the document, date of publication or of last revision, the URL, and your date of access.

A Web source:
> Shyovitz, David. "The History and Development of Yiddish." Jewish Virtual Library 30 May 2005 < http://www.jewishvirtuallibrary.org/jsource/ History/yiddish.html > .

Your teacher will tell you exactly how information should be cited in your essay. Generally, the very least information needed is the original author's name and the name of the article or other publication.

Be sure you know exactly what information your teacher requires before you start looking for your supporting information so that you know what information to include with your notes.

Sample Essay Topics

Subject: Is Illegal Immigration a Serious Problem?

Illegal Immigration Is a Drain on Government Resources

Illegal Immigration Is Not a Drain on Government Resources

Illegal Immigrants Contribute to American Society

Illegal Immigrants Do Not Contribute to American Society

Illegal Immigrants Take Jobs Away from Americans

Illegal Immigrants Take Jobs Americans Do Not Want to Do

Illegal Immigration Increases the Possibility of Terrorism

Illegal Immigration Does Not Increase the Possibility of Terrorism

Subject: How Can Illegal Immigration Be Reduced?

Illegal Immigrants Should Be Given Amnesty

Illegal Immigrants Should Not Be Given Amnesty

Guest Worker Programs Will Reduce Illegal Immigration

Guest Worker Programs Will Not Reduce Illegal Immigration

Increasing Legal Immigration Would End Illegal Immigration

Increasing Legal Immigration Would Not End Illegal Immigration

Citizen Patrols Can Help Reduce Illegal Immigration

Citizen Patrols Are the Wrong Way to Reduce Illegal Immigration

Organizations to Contact

American Civil Liberties Union (ACLU)
132 W. 43rd St., New York, NY 10036
(212) 944-9800
fax: (212) 921-7916
Web site: www.aclu.org

The ACLU is a national organization that champions the rights found in the Declaration of Independence and the U.S. Constitution. The ACLU Immigrants' Rights Project works with refugees and immigrants facing deportation, and with immigrants in the workplace. It has published reports, position papers, and a book, *The Rights of Aliens and Refugees*, that detail what freedoms immigrants and refugees have under the U.S. Constitution.

American Friends Service Committee (AFSC)
1501 Cherry St., Philadelphia, PA 19102
(215) 241-7000
fax: (215) 241-7275
e-mail: afscinfo@afsc.org
Web site: www.afsc.org

The AFSC is a Quaker organization that attempts to relieve human suffering and find new approaches to world peace and social justice through nonviolence. It lobbies against what it believes to be unfair immigration laws, especially sanctions criminalizing the employment of illegal immigrants. It has published *Sealing Our Borders: The Human Toll*, a report documenting human rights violations committed by law enforcement agents against immigrants.

American Immigration Control Foundation
PO Box 525, Monterey, VA 24465
(540) 468-2022
fax: (540) 468-2024
e-mail: aicfndn@cfw.com

Web site: www.aicfoundation.com

The AIC Foundation is an independent research and education organization that believes massive immigration, especially illegal immigration, is harming America. It calls for an end to illegal immigration and for stricter controls on legal immigration. The foundation's publications include *Erasing America: The Politics of the Borderless Nation*.

American Immigration Law Foundation (AILF)
918 F St. NW, 6th Fl., Washington, DC 20004
(202) 742-5600
fax: (202) 742-5619
e-mail: info@ailf.org
Web site: www.ailf.org

The American Immigration Law Foundation is an educational and charitable organization that seeks to increase public understanding of immigration law and of the contributions of immigrants to American society. Policy briefs, reports, and commentaries on legal and illegal immigration are available on the Web site. In addition, the *Immigration Policy Focus*, which publishes several times each year, provides analyses of immigration issues.

California Coalition for Immigration Reform (CCIR)
PO Box 2744-117, Huntington Beach, CA 92649
(714) 665-2500
fax: (714) 846-9682
Web site: www.ccir.net

CCIR is a grassroots volunteer organization representing Americans concerned with illegal immigration. It seeks to educate and inform the public and to effectively ensure enforcement of the nation's immigration laws. CCIR publishes alerts, bulletins, and the monthly newsletter *911*.

Center for Immigration Studies
1522 K St. NW, Suite 820, Washington, DC 20005-1202

(202) 466-8185
fax: (202) 466-8076
e-mail: center@cis.org
Web site: www.cis.org

The center studies the effects of immigration on the economic, social, demographic, and environmental conditions in the United States. It believes that the large number of recent immigrants has become a burden on America and favors reforming immigration laws to make them more consistent with U.S. interests. The center publishes editorials, reports, and position papers, such as "Crime & the Illegal Alien: The Fallout from Crippled Immigration Enforcement."

Federation for American Immigration Reform (FAIR)

1666 Connecticut Ave. NW, Suite 400
Washington, DC 20009
(202) 328-7004
fax: (202) 387-3447
e-mail: comments@fairus.org
Web site: www.fairus.org

FAIR works to stop illegal immigration and to limit legal immigration. It believes that the growing flood of immigrants into the United States causes higher unemployment and taxes social services. FAIR publishes a monthly newsletter, reports, and position papers, which are available on its Web site.

National Alliance Against Racist and Political Repression (NAARPR)

11 John St., Rm. 702, New York, NY 10038
(212) 406-3330
fax: (212) 406-3542

NAARPR is a coalition of political, labor, church, civic, student, and community organizations that opposes the many forms of human rights repression in the United

States. It seeks to end the harassment and deportation of illegal immigrant workers. The alliance publishes pamphlets and the quarterly newsletter, *Organizer*.

National Immigration Forum
220 I St. NE, Suite 220, Washington, DC 20002-4362
(202) 544-0004
fax: (202) 544-1905
Web site: www.immigrationforum.org

The forum believes that legal immigrants strengthen America and that welfare benefits do not attract illegal immigrants. It supports effective measures aimed at curbing illegal immigration and promotes programs and policies that help refugees and immigrants assimilate into American society. The forum publishes the quarterly newsletter *Golden Door* and the bimonthly newsletter *Immigration Policy Matters*.

Negative Population Growth, Inc. (NPG)
1717 Massachusetts Ave. NW, Suite 101
Washington, DC 20036
(202) 667-8950
fax: (202) 667-8953
e-mail: npg@npg.org
Web site: www.npg.org

NPG believes that world population must be reduced and that the United States is already overpopulated. It calls for an end to illegal immigration and an annual cap on legal immigration of two hundred thousand people. This would achieve "zero net migration" because two hundred thousand people exit the country each year, according to NPG. NPG frequently publishes position papers on population and immigration in its *NPG Forum*.

NumbersUSA.com
1601 N. Kent St., Suite 1100, Arlington, VA 22209
(703) 816-8820
e-mail: info@numbersusa.com

NumbersUSA.com is a nonpartisan public policy organization that aims to reduce the overall levels of immigration in order to achieve an environmentally sustainable and economically just United States. News articles, congressional testimony, and studies on immigration are among the materials available on the site.

U.S. Border Control (USBC)

8180 Greensboro Dr., Suite 1070, McLean, VA 22102
(703) 356-6568
fax: (202) 478-0254
e-mail: info@usbc.org
Web site: www.usbc.org

USBC is a lobbying group dedicated to ending illegal immigration by reforming U.S. immigration policies and securing American borders. It publishes articles on U.S. border and immigration policies in its newsletter *Border Alert* and on its Web site.

U.S. Citizenship and Immigration Service (USCIS)

U.S. Department of Homeland Security
Washington, DC 20528
Web site: www.uscis.gov

The USCIS, an agency of the Department of Homeland Defense, took over the functions and responsibilities of the former Immigration and Naturalization Service, including the enforcement of immigration laws and regulations. It produces numerous reports and evaluations on selected programs. Statistics and information on immigration and immigration laws and other materials are available on its Web site.

Bibliography

Books

Cole, David, *Enemy Aliens: Double Standards and Constitutional Freedoms in the War on Terrorism*. New York: New Press, 2003.

Daniels, Roger, *Guarding the Golden Door: American Immigration Policy and Immigrants Since 1882*. New York: Hill and Wang, 2004.

Davis, Mike, and Justin Akers Chacon, *No One Is Illegal: Fighting Racism and State Violence on the U.S.-Mexico Border*. Chicago: Haymarket, 2006.

Dougherty, Jon E., *Illegals: The Imminent Threat Posed by Our Unsecured U.S.-Mexico Border*. Nashville: WND, 2004.

Gelletly, Lee Anne, *Mexican Immigration*. Philadelphia: Mason Crest, 2004.

Hanson, Victor Davis, *Mexifornia: A State of Becoming*. San Francisco: Encounter, 2003.

Hayworth, J.D., *Whatever It Takes: Illegal Immigration, Border Security, and the War on Terror*. Washington, DC: Regnery, 2006.

Hunter, Miranda, *Latino Americans and Immigration Laws: Crossing the Border*. Philadelphia: Mason Crest, 2006.

Krauss, Erich, *On the Line: Inside the U.S. Border Patrol*. New York: Citadel, 2004.

LeMay, Michael C., *U.S. Immigration: A Reference Handbook*. Santa Barbara, CA: ABC-CLIO, 2004.

Malkin, Michelle, *Invasion: How America Still Welcomes Terrorists, Criminals, and Other Foreign Menaces to Our Shores*. Washington, DC: Regnery, 2002.

Martinez, Ruben, *Crossing Over: A Mexican Family on the Migrant Trail*. New York: Picador, 2002.

Massey, Douglas S., Jorge Durand, and Nolan J. Malone, *Beyond Smoke and Mirrors: Mexican Immigration in an Era of Economic Integration*. New York: Russell Sage Foundation, 2002.

Nazario, Sonia, *Enrique's Journey*. New York: Random House, 2006.

Nevins, Joseph, *Operation Gatekeeper: The Rise of the "Illegal Alien" and the Remaking of the U.S.-Mexico Boundary*. New York: Routledge, 2002.

Ramos, Jorge, *Dying to Cross: The Worst Immigrant Tragedy in American History*. Trans. Kristina Cordero. New York: Rayo, 2005.

Tancredo, Tom, *Open Borders, Open Wounds: What America Needs to Know About Illegal Immigration*. San Francisco: Encounter, 2005.

Urrea, Luis Alberto, *The Devil's Highway: A True Story*. New York: Little, Brown, 2004.

Periodicals

Barlett, Donald L., and James Steele, "Who Left the Door Open?" *Time*, September 20, 2004.

Boyce, Geoffrey, "Cynicism on the U.S./Mexico Border," *Z Magazine*, December 2005.

Castañeda, Jorge, "Addition to the Melting Pot Requires a New Recipe Book," *Los Angeles Times*, April 2, 2004.

Cooper, Marc, "The 15-Second Men," *Los Angeles Times*, May 1, 2005.

Current Events, "Deadly Crossings," April 22, 2005.

Downing, Renee, "Border Control?" *Washington Post*, national weekly ed., May 9, 2005.

Duignan, Peter, "Do Immigrants Benefit America?" *World and I*, February 2004.

Edwards, James R., "The Cost of Immigration," *Chronicles*, February 2004.

Francis, Samuel, "Are Terrorists Crossing Our Borders?" *Conservative Chronicle*, November 3, 2004.

Griswold, Daniel, "Mexican Workers Come Here to Work: Let Them!" *Wall Street Journal*, October 22, 2002.

Issues and Controversies on File, "Noncitizen Voting Rights," September 17, 2004.

Jacoby, Tamar, "Borderline—Why We Can't Stop Illegal Immigration," *New Republic*, January 26, 2004.

King, William, interviewed by William F. Jasper, "We *Can* Control Our Borders," *New American*, January 23, 2006.

Lin, Rong-Gong, "Mexican Immigrants Not Burdening ERs, Study Says," *Los Angeles Times*, October 14, 2005.

McCarthy, Terry, "Stalking the Day Laborers," *Time*, December 5, 2005.

Moore, Stephen, "More Immigrants, More Jobs," *Wall Street Journal*, July 11, 2005.

National Catholic Reporter, "The Immigration Dilemma," January 13, 2006.

Page, Clarence, "Our Make-Believe Immigration Policy," *Liberal Opinion Week*, May 25, 2005.

Phyllis Schlafly Report, "Conservative Agenda for 2005: Stop Entry of Illegal Aliens," January 2005.

Triplett, William, "Migrant Farmworkers," *CQ Researcher*, October 8, 2004.

Web Sites

American Border Patrol (www.americanborderpatrol. com). An anti–illegal immigration organization whose members use high-tech equipment to detect, locate, and report illegal immigration as it occurs. American Border Patrol members do not physically interfere with illegals, but do observe and report them to government authorities. Their

Web site contains articles about illegal immigration and many aerial photos of border regions.

El Rescate (www.elrescate.org). El Rescate provides free legal and social services to Central American refugees. It is involved in federal litigation to uphold the constitutional rights of refugees and illegal immigrants. It compiles and distributes articles and information and publishes the newsletter *El Rescate*.

Illegal Immigrants.us (www.illegalaliens.us). A conservative organization whose goal is to provide information on illegal immigration prevention, enforcement, and attrition. The Web site contains links to articles, polls, statistics, blogs, and other resources regarding illegal immigration.

National Network for Immigrant and Refugee Rights (www.nnirr.org). The network includes community, church, labor, and legal groups committed to the cause of equal rights for all immigrants. These groups work to end discrimination and unfair treatment of illegal immigrants and refugees. Its Web site contains reports and the monthly newsletter *Network News*.

Index

Allied Communities of
   Tarrant, 51–52
American dream, 39
amnesty, 73–78
Asian population, 32
assimilation, 33–34
automation, 28, 30

births, 47–48
border, 32
Boudreaux, Richard, 13
Buchanan, Pat, 31, 59

Camarota, Steven A., 18,
   58–59
Campo Flores, Ariana, 67
Center for Immigration
   Studies, 18
Comprehensive
   Immigration Reform
   Act, 73–74
"Coyotes," 14–15
crime, 66–69
crossing border, 14–16
current Population
   Survey, 23

Davidson, Adam, 25, 59
disease, 43–46
dropouts, 20, 27
dysentery, 44

economy, 29–30
education, 20–22
employer sponsorship,
   11–12
employment 23–24
ethnic entitlements,
   32–33

Federation for American
   Immigration Reform
   (FAIR), 42, 50, 51, 59

gang activity, 67–68
Gonzales, Richard J., 49
Grigg, William Norman,
   67

Haiti, 14
health insurance, 46–47,
   51
Hispanic population, 32
immigration law, 39
Immigration Reform and
   Control Act, 76
incarceration, 68

Jacoby, Jeff, 36
jobs, 18–24

labor shortage crisis,
   75–76

legal immigration,
 11–12, 37–39
leprosy, 44, 45

Malvo, Lee Boyd, 66, 68
medical care
 barriers to access to,
  54
 costs of, 45–48, 50–51,
  52–53
 denial of, 51–52
 provision of, 52
"melting pot," 11, 41
Mexico
 minimum wage in, 12
 remittance to, 13
 soccer games in, 34
MS-13, 67–68
Muhammad, John Allen,
 66
multiculturalism, 34,
 40–41

outpatient treatment,
 51–52

political refugees, 12,
 13–14
Pomfret, John, 14–15
population
 boom, 77
 of illegal residents, 11
 of white Americans, 32

of working adults, 19
pork tapeworm, 45
public services, 74–75

quality of life, 12

racial preferences,
 32–33
Rector, Robert, 76, 77
refugee status, 12,
 13–14
relatives, 11, 77
remittance, 13
risk-takers, 39

self-starters, 39

tuberculosis, 44, 46
typhoid, 45

unemployment rates, 27
unskilled work force, 21
Urban Institute, 67

wages
 impact on, 26–27
 in major cities, 27–28
 in Mexico compared to
  in United States,
  12–13
West Nile virus, 45
workforce, illegal immi-
 grants in, 22–23

Picture Credits

About the Editor

San Diego resident Laura K. Egendorf received her B.A. in English from Wesleyan University. A book editor for the past nine years, she is especially interested in books that explore free speech or popular culture. When she is not working, Laura's interests include food, sports, music, and trivia.